Ellen Spencer Mussey at 75.

FATE RIDES A TORTOISE

A Biography of

ELLEN SPENCER MUSSEY

By

GRACE HATHAWAY

THE JOHN C. WINSTON COMPANY

CHICAGO *Philadelphia* TORONTO

DEDICATED
TO WOMEN

NOTE

This book is an attempt to give a true picture of Ellen Spencer Mussey's life and times, with particular emphasis upon the struggles of women in their new ventures and the public reaction to those ventures. The story is a result of conversations with Mrs. Mussey and those who knew her.

Especially helpful in supplying information for the book were Miss Florence C. Bell, Miss Laura M. Berrien, Mrs. Burnita Shelton Matthews, Judge Mary O'Toole, Miss Katharine Pike, Mrs. Helena Doocy Reed, Mrs. Grace Hays Riley, Dean of the Washington College of Law; Judge Kathryn Sellers, Miss Lucilla Smith, Dr. William Tindall, Mrs. Mary E. Wells, and Miss Emma Wold.

Other sources of information were:

American National Red Cross Relief Committee Reports.

Blackwell, Alice Stone, *Lucy Stone.*

Bryan, Wilhelmus Bogart, *A History of the National Capital.*

Colman, Edna M., *White House Gossip.*

Congressional Record.

Equal Rights (Independent Feminist Weekly).

Harper, Ida Husted, *The Life and Works of Susan B. Anthony.*

Haskin, Frederic J., *The American Government.*

Howe, Henry, *Historical Collections of Ohio.*

Irwin, Inez Haynes, *Angels and Amazons.*

Laws and Ordinances of the Public Health—1881.

Leanord, Delaven L., *Oberlin College.*

Lineage Books of the National Society of Daughters of Founders and Patriots of America.

Lossing, John B., *Matthew Vassar, 1792-1868.*

Pamphlets of the League of Women Voters.

Paul, Nanette B., *The Great Woman Statesman.*

Singleton, Esther, *The Story of the White House.*

Stevens, Doris, *Jailed for Freedom.*

The Biographical Cyclopaedia of American Women.
The *Evening Star.*
Tindall, William, *Standard History of the City of Washington.*
Twain, Mark, *Joan of Arc.*
Washington College of Law Files.
Washington Daily News.
Washington Herald.
Washington Post.
Washington Times.

G. H.

CONTENTS

ILLUSTRATIONS

Chapter I

EARLY DAYS IN OHIO

Persis Duty was warned not to marry Platt Spencer. By his own sister, too. Platt Spencer was the spoiled youngest of a family of twelve, and at twenty-eight he was still too fond of good times, too unsettled to undertake the responsibilities of a family, his sister thought.

But the black-eyed, rosy-cheeked Persis loved him. He was so companionable and witty, so handsomely blue-eyed. Besides, he had an amazing genius for penmanship. In all the countryside no one could write with such beauty and flourish as Platt Spencer, and people came from far and near to watch him and learn from him. As for his failings, young Persis was sure she could manage them. She was the eldest of her family; she had brought up six motherless brothers and sisters and responsibilities held no terrors for her. She would simply marry her young man and reform him.

And with all the confidence and high courage of twenty-two, she became Platt Spencer's wife in Ashtabula, Ohio, in 1828. Fortunately, in the warp and woof of her being was the stuff of pioneers used to wrestling with odds, and through her veins coursed the blood of two grandfathers who had fought in the War of the Revolution.

After all, young Persis was following somewhat of a precedent, for her own mother, who had been Miss Sally Warren, had married in the face of opposition. Of a fine, wealthy family, she had given her love to poor, unreliable, but handsome and captivating Ebenezer Duty. Such a remarkable physique had he, such strength, it was said he could lift a ton.

Ebenezer and Sally Duty were natives of New Hampshire but some years after their marriage they had come by ox-team and covered wagon to seek opportunity in the Western

Reserve. And Sally's father, Moses Warren, fearing to trust his daughter and her small children to the care of Ebenezer, had accompanied them. Mr. Warren rode horseback all the way from New Hampshire.

At night they had stopped at farm houses rather than sleep in their wagons, as many emigrants did, for Father Warren believed in having as much comfort and safety as possible. When the Dutys had been established on a farm near Lake Erie, Mr. Warren made the long journey back to New Hampshire to get his own family. The new Ohio country was full of promise, and colonists were flocking westward. They came from all parts of the eastern seaboard and, among those from New York State, was the family of Platt Spencer.

The Spencer forbears had been Cromwellians and had come in the early days to settle in Rhode Island. John Spencer, the Colonial ancestor, had been town clerk, "Conservator of the Peace," and Deputy to the General Court in East Greenwich, R. I. Caleb Spencer, who was Platt's father, had served in the Revolutionary War and had married a young widow, Jerusha Covell, of Chatham, Cape Cod, the night before he marched to join his regiment. When he came home again his body was scarred by sabre cuts, striking evidence of the hand-to-hand fighting of the times.

After the war Caleb and his family had gone to Dutchess County, N. Y., and later to East Windham in Greene County, where he died when Platt was six years old. A few years later the Widow Spencer with her children made the long trek by ox-team to Ohio and settled on the shore of Lake Erie near Ashtabula.

Before he was six years old little Platt revealed a critical attitude toward the ugliness of the disjointed, labored penmanship of the day, visioned a script in a fine, free-flowing movement and worked doggedly to give form to his ideas. Lacking paper he wrote on the uncolored sides of leather at the tanneries near his home, using dye for ink. In Ohio he found the shore of Lake Erie an ideal place to practice and, with the aid of a stick, he learned to write smoothly for half a mile in the sand. As a young man he did some teaching and worked at various jobs. But a great deal of his time was passed in the corner grocery store.

The grocery was the club room of the community where men gathered to loaf and talk. And Platt Spencer with his eloquence and wit, his skill in drawing and fine penmanship, was the life of the crowd. Marriage brought no change in his habits.

When the first child, Robert, was born, and Spencer still showed no signs of settling down, young Mrs. Spencer began to worry and, in the hope that leaving Ashtabula might be helpful, she prevailed upon her husband to take up farming on the lake shore.

A second child was born, but it died within a few months. The farm did not prosper because Spencer passed most of his time with his friends in town. By and by through his penmanship work came an invitation to go to New York City. He accepted, and Mrs. Spencer, soon to become a mother for the third time, got a job teaching the district school and looked after herself and her son, Robert, as best she could. Part of the time she lived in the schoolhouse, enduring privation and discomfort.

Mr. Spencer was gone a long time. He stopped at town after town on his way to and from New York and he had a good time. When he finally returned home he showed not the slightest compunction for his neglect. Exhilarated by his journey, he did not even seem aware that he had been neglectful.

It was the proverbial last straw for Persis Duty Spencer. The spirit of her fighting ancestry thoroughly aroused, she turned furiously upon Platt Spencer and gave him her ultimatum. He must settle down to his family responsibilities or she would leave him.

This sudden outburst of passion must have been somewhat cataclysmic in its effect, or perhaps in this new and unexpected Persis, Spencer glimpsed the prospect of something eminently more desirable than what he had perceived in the past. At any rate he gave her his solemn promise to shoulder his responsibilities and go to work in earnest.

Both of them knew reform would come easier among new scenes and new faces and they moved to a farm on Indian Creek where associates were better, outdoor life attractive. Spencer kept his promise, and they prospered, moving to better and better farms. Other children were born to them, and by and by they bought a farm three miles from Geneva, Ohio, where they built a fine large home for their growing family.

Besides farming, Spencer served as Treasurer of Ashtabula County and worked diligently in perfecting the Spencerian System of Penmanship, which was becoming famous throughout the country. He also became an ardent advocate of temperance and lectured and wrote for the cause.

When Platt Spencer was fifty years of age and Mrs. Spencer forty-four, their tenth child, Persis Ellen Spencer, was born, May 13, 1850. The new arrival was hailed with delight, for large families were the fashion and Mrs. Spencer was very proud of having given birth to ten children. But two of them had died in infancy and the new baby was frail and sickly. Her parents feared she would not survive babyhood.

Two hundred acres of land near the southern shore of Lake Erie, half of it in woods of maple, oak, beech, and chestnut; gardens, fruit, grain fields, barns; a big white house with honeysuckle vines, lilacs, and shade trees of maple and locust; a creek curving across the back yard; a grove for picnics and another creek with an artificial lake for boating; that was the Spencer farm.

It was well stocked with horses, cows, hogs, sheep, and chickens, but there were no geese or ducks. They injured the soil Mr. Spencer believed, as did many other farmers.

The house was near the road with four rooms across the front, three of them, the parlor, sitting room, and kitchen,

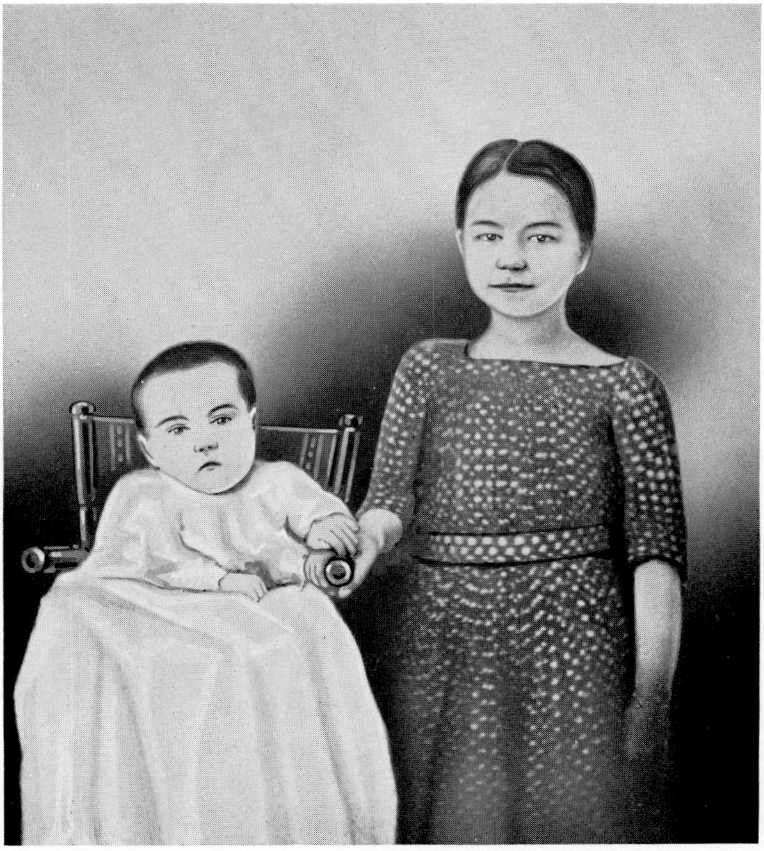

Ellen Spencer, age three months, with her sister, Phoebe.

having front doors. Mr. Spencer's office was next to the kitchen and, since activities centered about these two rooms, visitors usually came to the kitchen front door.

At the back were bedrooms, a porch, the buttery, and upstairs more bedrooms as well as a dark room for storage purposes. The house was enclosed in a yard with a white-washed fence, and narrow pebbled walks led in half circles to each of the front doors.

At one end of the house where there was a commanding view of the road, the dog, Trim, had his kennel, and Trim heralded all travelers lustily and persistently. But travelers were few, permitting much canine indolence, and then Trim was apt to seek shelter and companionship within the house. Long deep grooves were worn in the panels of the back door where he had scratched for admission, but he knew he dared not scratch at any of the three front doors.

Across the road from the house was a log cabin which Mr. Spencer called "Jericho" and there he taught penmanship. His writing with its smooth-flowing capitals, its beautiful flourishes and shadings, and his graceful swirling pen pictures of birds, trees, and landscapes, had won for him an immense popularity. Everybody wanted to learn the Spencerian System, and students came from all parts of the country.

They took lessons, too, by correspondence, and one student, a California gold miner, paid for his course in gold dust, sent across the continent in little chamois bags. Penmanship classes began to spring up throughout the country. Penmanship was the fashion. Besides, typewriters were as yet unheard of, and a good hand was a business asset. All the Spencer children, Robert, Sara, Platt, Jr., the twins, Harvey and Henry, Lyman, and Phoebe, who was eight, had had to begin early to learn the Spencerian principles.

The new baby, Nellie or Ella as they called her depending on the mood of the moment, was a fragile, black-eyed mite, always ill with colds or digestive troubles. But the family lavished her with care, and somehow she struggled through infancy and began to grow a little stronger. Still she was often sick and her earliest memories were associated with the ailments of her childhood.

One morning when she was three or four years old she awoke ill and miserable with the toothache. Though it was very early Mrs. Spencer was already up, and Nellie in her nightgown hurried to the kitchen to find her mother. To the child's amazement, there behind the kitchen stove stood a huge black man. His eyes rolled at sight of the little girl. Nellie had never before seen a black man and fascinated, forgetful of toothache, she watched him.

"Nellie," warned her mother, "you must not stand there in your bare feet. Get into your cart." The black man said he would help "Little Missy" and he tucked her gently into the cart.

She liked being called "Little Missy" and she was filled with questions about this strange, nice black man. But her mother merely said that he had come to be with them for a while. Suddenly, a few days later he was gone, and Nellie, troubled about it, was told that he had gone to visit other folks. The Spencers were fervent abolitionists. Their home was part of the underground railroad, and they helped many slaves on their way north.

When Nellie was four years old her father began giving her lessons in penmanship. She was so little that her chair had to be placed on a platform so that she could reach the table. She did not want to learn to write because it was a painful task, but Mr. Spencer was a persuasive teacher. He gave her beautiful copies to follow and told her stories of the letters, that the pebble on the beach had been his copy for the ovals and that he had patterned the m's and n's after the notched edges of leaves. Patiently he taught her the free-arm movement with the hand resting on the nails of the third and fourth fingers. From the beginning she wrote with pen and ink and when she had done well, he rewarded her with gold pens.

She was very proud of her first letter written at the age of five to her eldest brother, Robert, who was ill in Buffalo.

"Dear Brother Robert

I am sorry you are sick. I want you to be well again. I send a kiss, Dear Brother. Goodbye Dear Brother. hope you will soon be home.

Your sister Ella"

Caring for Robert entailed considerable expense and little Nellie wanted to help. She had some money, an English shilling and a German kreutzer, and her father wrote to Robert:

"Nellie comes now with an earnest and special request that she may be permitted to send the shilling to Robert. I proposed that she send the kreutzer instead but she replies that 'the shilling is worth a great deal the most'. So you see she is anxious to send her most valuable treasure. Accept it from the dear little prattler. . . ."

Nellie loved stories and she learned to read by watching the page while others of the family read to her. Children's books were few but she read and reread the popular blue and gold books by Fanny Fern. The little girl received much of her early instruction at home, partly because she was not strong and the school was a long distance away, and partly because district school teachers at the time had very little training.

But other children of the neighborhood went to school and Nellie begged so hard to go with them that finally her parents consented and she attended the school for two terms. It made her intensely happy to be with children of her own age and every morning she met her schoolmates at the crossroads.

They carried their lunches in round tin pails and all the children brought green onions except Nellie. Green onions suddenly became very desirable. Nellie coaxed to have green onions in her lunch. But her mother refused. "They would smell up your whole lunch," she said.

The other children went barefoot to school but Nellie, because she took cold so easily, had to wear shoes and stockings even on the hottest days. Her playmates made fun of her. Life seemed very, very difficult.

One morning shortly before her sixth birthday Nellie was sent to visit a little neighbor girl, Helen Woodward, and they played all day with Helen's corncob dolls. When Nellie returned home she found a new black-eyed baby sister. She was overjoyed because now she would have a playmate all her own. The baby was named Emma.

That same year Nellie had her first journey, a visit to Cleveland with her father and mother. Her special pride for the occasion was a pair of new gray silk gloves but they were somewhat large and had to be tied on with bright blue ribbons.

Before reaching Cleveland the train crossed a high trestle and Nellie, looking down, saw people far below her. They looked very tiny, and turning excitedly to her father she asked, "Why are the people here so little?"

The Spencers attended the Baptist church in Geneva, or rather Mrs. Spencer and the children did. Mr. Spencer had left the church because one of the deacons was continually getting drunk and nothing was done about it.

Every winter the church held revival services, an evangelist gave rousing sermons, and there was a great deal of testifying. Nellie at the age of eight was converted. Her parents thought she was too young to join the church, but she was very serious about it and insisted upon being baptised.

To her that was a thrilling ceremony. It was held at night with the church brightly lighted, a special font built under the pulpit, stirring music, and a great crowd of people. It was a bitter winter night, too, and Mrs. Spencer feared Nellie would take cold. But she was hurried into dry clothes immediately after the immersion and no illness resulted.

According to the custom of the times, the pastor of the church called regularly upon the members of his congregation, and when he went to the Spencers he usually arrived in the morning and stayed for the day. That meant chickens must be killed for dinner. There was always a great bustling to have the best of everything for the minister.

But his visits were a sore trial to young Nellie, because

part of the ministerial duty of the day was to remind his host and hostess of their sins and to ask each child peremptorily if he or she loved the Lord. Nellie, shy and sensitive, shrank before this questioning, and one day when she saw the minister drive up to the gate, she ran and hid under a guest room bed. She was soon found, however. Everyone had to be on hand to pay respects to the minister.

The Spencers had a great deal of company. Besides relatives and friends there were teachers and students and homeless folk whom Mrs. Spencer took in because they had no place else to go. At times she took in sick people and nursed them. A neighbor woman came to be cured of the drug habit. A cousin came afflicted with delirium tremens. And now and then Mrs. Spencer entertained inmates of the county poor farm for a week or two at a time.

One of these visitors was known as "Crazy Dudley," a silent man who sat hour after hour in a corner of the sitting room. He excited Nellie's curiosity, and one day when everyone else was outside, she stayed in the sitting room and walked back and forth watching Crazy Dudley.

Suddenly he exclaimed, "What beautiful eyes that girl has."

Nellie's heart raced with the thrill of that. She longed to be pretty. She had her mother's rosy cheeks and dimples, her mother's dark hair and eyes, and she had heard her father say, using his favorite expletive, "I Jarge, your mother is a fine looking woman!" but no one had ever told Nellie that she was fine looking or pretty and now at last she knew that she was. Breathless with excitement, she hurried outside and, seeing one of her brothers, exultantly told him what Crazy Dudley had said.

Her brother roared with laughter, then he told the other boys and they laughed and laughed. Never before, it seemed, had they heard such a tremendously funny joke. They told her to pay no attention to anything Crazy Dudley said, that she must remember he was crazy.

She returned to the house, convinced that she must be very ugly. She worried about it. But years later when she confessed this to her brothers, they said, "Oh, we thought you were very pretty but we did not want to make you vain."

Sometimes engravers came to the Spencer home to prepare the plates from which penmanship copies were to be made and, since it was difficult to get Americans with training and experience for this work, Mr. Spencer usually had it done by foreigners. And these foreign engravers, unaccustomed to the life of the country, were choice subjects for the Spencer boys' fun.

One day they took an Irish engraver rabbit hunting and brought him back to the house, bearing triumphantly an Ohio "rabbit," a pretty little black and white creature that filled the air with noisome odor. But Mrs. Spencer soon took a hand in this particular prank. Spencer, however, celebrated it by putting it into verse. He was fond of writing verses.

The Spencer home was somewhat of a neighborhood center. Communication was slow and difficult, there were no telephones, no rural free delivery of mail, and a great many people did not get newspapers. But the Spencers took a Cleveland paper, drove to Geneva daily to get it along with the other mail that came on the accommodation train, and after supper neighbors stopped in to hear the news. One day Mr. Spencer received a telegram, the first to come to that vicinity, and everyone was eager to hear about this swift new means of communication.

But among those who visited the Spencer home either on business or pleasure, not one was a lawyer. All lawyers in Mr. Spencer's opinion were shysters, and he would have nothing whatever to do with them. One of the boys, Harvey, studied law for a short time in Geneva, but his father protested so hotly that Harvey finally gave it up. To the family, however, this was merely one of Mr. Spencer's eccentricities. He was extreme about many things.

He would not tolerate anyone who thought himself above physical labor, and whenever a young man came to study penmanship Spencer applied an unique test. He invited the young man to go ditching in the rain. If he refused, he was not encouraged to remain for any further instruction, but if he accepted, he could consider himself in high favor with his instructor.

Spencer was eccentric about his food, too. He had always suffered from digestive troubles and he would not eat seleratus biscuits, hot breads of any kind, or preserves. He would not allow mince pies in the house and black pepper he classed as poison. But he used a great deal of red pepper.

Sometimes his sons played tricks on him and filled the pepper box with black pepper, but no sooner did he discover it, than out would go the pepper box, into the road as like as not. One day a passing neighbor found it. "Looks like some of the children have been playing with the pepper," he exclaimed. But he knew who had thrown it there. Everybody knew of Platt Spencer's peculiarities.

His curative for all ailments was castor oil and he took this mixed with his morning porridge. He liked being spectacular.

In one ear he wore a tiny circlet of gold wire. As a child he had suffered with inflammation of the eyes caused by too much reading in poor light and to cure this his grandmother had had his ears pierced and gold wires inserted. He must always wear them, she told him, to prevent any further trouble with his eyes. But one of the wires had somehow been lost.

Mr. Spencer attended to much of his penmanship work in the evening after the neighbors had gone, and to get into the proper frame of mind he liked to have his hair combed. Often it was Nellie who performed this service for her father and, while she sat on the table beside him combing his hair, he recited poems or told her stories. She loved these evenings. No one seemed to know as many interesting things as her father, no one was so lively and gay. They became close comrades. But sometimes others of the family objected that Nellie, young as she was, should be kept up so late.

Mr. Spencer taught penmanship in towns and cities throughout Ohio and nearby states and helped to found business colleges that were springing up over the country, for penmanship was one of the major subjects. When he went to Buffalo to give a course of instruction to the public school teachers, Mrs. Spencer accompanied him and they were presented with a pair of silver napkin rings.

But the Spencers did not have napkins, so the napkin rings were displayed as ornaments. A little later, Sara, the eldest daughter, bought napkins in Cleveland. Sara often brought home luxuries. One of them was loaf sugar so hard that a hammer had to be used to break it into bits.

Some of the sugar that the Spencers used was produced in their own maple grove and the sugar season was an exciting time for Nellie. She must always go with the boys, on the bobsled if it were snowy, or the wagon if it were mild, to collect the buckets of sap. They boiled it in a huge cauldron over a fire in the woods. After that, what they called "sugaring off" was done at night over the kitchen stove.

Everybody was on hand for that because everybody wanted to sample the finished product. In fact, so much was eaten Mr. Spencer was wont to complain that with all their trees they didn't have any more sugar than Mr. A———, a notoriously stingy neighbor, might get from his fence rails.

Another seasonal job was candle making. Candles furnished the light for the Spencer home and every fall as soon as the weather was cool, the year's supply was made. Candles were dipped, a long tedious process with wicks and melted tallow. Later some of the candles were molded, especially those for company use, but Mrs. Spencer did not think highly of this new-fangled method. Of course it took less time to mold candles and they looked prettier but she was sure they did not last as long as the dipped ones.

A row of candlesticks of tin, brass, and china was kept on a buttery shelf and one of the morning jobs was to clean them and put in new candles in preparation for the night.

There were days of endless chores. But the Spencers played, too. They had picnics in the maple grove and went rowing on the little artificial lake, in boats the boys had built. Occasionally, when the weather was fine on Saturday afternoon, they drove to the beach on Lake Erie and went swimming. But no one had bathing suits. Old clothes were kept for this purpose.

The important and really festive occasion of the whole year was the Fourth of July. Then people from all the countryside gathered at the lake shore. Nellie loved this holiday and was nearly always the first one up in the morning, a bundle of excitement, breathlessly eager to begin the day's events.

Fourth of July celebrations meant huge baskets of lunch, gallons and gallons of lemonade, and rows and rows of big frosted cakes. There was always a program, too, with patriotic speeches and singing. Often Mr. Spencer was the chief speaker of the day and he stirred the crowd with his oratory and wit. Nellie was immensely proud of him.

But it did not occur to her that she, too, might one day talk from the platform. She had never heard a woman speak. Therefore, it must be that women did not make speeches.

As a matter of fact, a few of the more daring ones had begun to make public speeches some time before this. Until 1828, however, it was virtually unheard of and to most people unthinkable for a woman to express herself in public except in the strictly feminine prayer meeting or a Quaker meeting.

But in 1828 Frances Wright, of Scotland, had come to this country and spoken on the public platform. A few years later America had its own pioneers, among them Sarah and Angelina Grimke, of South Carolina, and Abby Kelley Foster, of Massachusetts, who devoted themselves chiefly to antislavery topics.

These women were scorned and mobbed for the sin of speaking in public. They were considered unsexed. One church organization, learning of their activities, ordered its ministers not to permit "females" to speak in their churches. Mrs. Foster was branded a "Jezebel," a "servant of Satan," and, according to one account, men and women found guilty of listening to her speeches were expelled from church.

When Susan B. Anthony, in 1853, asked to speak at a teachers' meeting, something no woman had done despite the large number of women teaching, the men in charge were aghast and had to discuss the matter some time before they gave her permission to talk. Afterward, many of the women drew aside from Miss Anthony and vented their scorn upon her "disgraceful performance."

But, as the years passed, more and more women braved contempt, ridicule, and Biblical injunction to make public speeches. It was a long time, however, before the practice became sufficiently common to give the average person an opportunity to hear a woman make a speech and the idea persisted that it was the men who should make speeches.

Chapter II

RESPONSIBILITIES AT A TENDER AGE

The Spencers wanted to give their children as many educational advantages as possible and for the benefit of the younger members of the family they left the farm in 1859 and moved to Oberlin, Ohio. Mr. Spencer established a penmanship school, Lyman and Phoebe attended Oberlin College, and Nellie went to the grade school.

Oberlin College was radical and had been radical and sensational from its beginning. Founded in 1833, it had admitted women on the same terms as men, the first college in the country to dare such an extraordinary innovation. Among its famous students had been Lucy Stone, feminist and lecturer, and Antoinette L. Brown, first woman to be ordained as a minister. Lucy Stone had studied Greek to find out among other things about that oft-repeated injunction of St. Paul, "Let your women keep silence in the churches," and she had learned that what he actually said was, "Let your women not gabble in the churches," which was considerably different.

For all its liberality in admitting women, Oberlin had many restrictions. Women were not allowed to take part in debates though that was part of the regular work of the men students, and women could take no vocal part in commencement exercises with the men though they might write pieces to be read by one of the professors.

So intense was the feeling against women speaking in public that Lucy Stone and a few other young women, eager for some practice in the art, met secretly in the woods and made speeches while sentinels kept watch for intruders. When Antoinette Brown wanted to enter the theological school, faculty members were dismayed and held many conferences before finally agreeing to admit her. But for many years after her graduation, her name was withheld from the list of the theological school, simply because she was a woman.

Oberlin College also admitted Negroes on equal terms with whites and thereby brought upon itself an avalanche of condemnation. The town welcomed escaped slaves. It boasted of its ability to outwit slave catchers and claimed that no slave who came there was ever carried back into bondage. There was scarcely a house that had not harbored fleeing slaves. Oberlin gloried in its principles.

But elsewhere Oberlin was held in contempt. Threats were made to burn the college buildings. Legislators agitated the question of repealing the college charter. Even its close neighbors considered Oberlin fanatic, and a sign board pointing the way to the town, pictured the full-length figure of a fugitive slave.

Oberlin College was devoted to religious principles and, in its early days, teachers and students had practiced extreme self-denial to provide money for Christian work. It had been the belief of certain earnest leaders that if convicts could live on bread and water, so could students, and food had been reduced to a minimum. One diet in vogue had been Graham bread, thin gravy, and salt. Later it had been suggested that even more money might be saved for Christian beneficence if parched corn were substituted for Graham bread. But this proposal had met with no enthusiasm, and by and by more normal diets were resumed.

Oberlin leaders in their zeal were often astonishing but none was more so than Mr. C. G. Finney, President of the College. An inveterate evangelist was Mr. Finney. In the midst of the most casual remarks, on the street or anywhere, he was wont to ask people about their souls and if they loved the Lord. Meeting a student one evening after a fire in the town, President Finney said, "Good evening! That was a bad fire, wasn't it? Are you a Christian?"

Once Nellie Spencer met President Finney out walking and, as he looked sternly down at her, he demanded, "Little girl, do you love the Lord?" She was too startled to answer.

Mr. Finney was a very practical man, too. The daily life of his people—a neighbor borrowing too many tools, an organization going into debt—these things were the subjects of his discourses. With pungency he preached and he prayed. A prayer for rain became the talk of the town.

The drought had been long and severe but clouds had gathered overhead in a black threatening mass and Mr. Finney petitioned the Lord to let them pour forth their waters and deluge the earth. "Let them not pass over and discharge their water upon the lake as they have so often done of late," he urged, "for thou knowest there is already water enough in the lake."

It rained that day in Oberlin.

At the grade school, Nellie studied Latin. Her father wanted her to be a Latin scholar and dutifully she conjugated verbs. But it was a meaningless subject, and she hated it. Still, to please her father, she kept on with it.

Life now began to assume more serious aspects. For some time Mrs. Spencer had not been well. So many babies, so many years of endless labors for those about her, had exhausted her energies, and the effort of getting settled in a new home, eager as she had been to do this, caused a complete physical breakdown.

Absolute rest was imperative and the responsibilities of the home had to be taken over by other members of the family. Nellie, aged nine, who had already shown a tendency to be practical, was assigned to do the family marketing. Her father gave her money, offered suggestions, and left the rest to her.

Often she made mistakes, but Mr. Spencer was gentle in pointing out errors and, when she had done well, he praised her highly. Soon she was buying all the household necessities, selecting her own clothes, and attending to the needs of her little sister, Emma. Nellie took great pride in helping.

But Mrs. Spencer's health did not improve and at the end of two years the Spencers, hopeful that a change might be beneficial, left Oberlin and returned to the farm. They arrived in Geneva two weeks before the firing upon Fort Sumter.

When the Civil War began, Harvey Spencer was in Winchester, Tennessee, visiting his cousins, Mr. and Mrs. Graves, the former, President of Mary Sharp College for Women. It was known that Harvey was the son of an abolitionist, he was warned to leave town, and the family feared for his safety. But Mrs. Graves, in order to prevent an attack upon the young man, accompanied him to the station and he arrived home without difficulty.

The Spencer boys were eager to get into the fray. Robert enlisted at once for three months. Everyone was sure the war would be over at the end of that time. Henry was mustered in but later discharged because of physical disabilities. Platt, Jr., had an invalid wife and he sent a substitute. Lyman at first was refused because of physical disabilities but later was accepted for clerical services and assigned to military duty.

It was a time of excitement and uncertainty and Mrs. Spencer through anxiety for her boys, failed rapidly. She died August, 1862.

Nellie was grief-stricken. And confronted by this strange and incomprehensible void, she clung more than ever to her father. Though she was very young, she wore mourning. That was the custom but because of her extreme youth she wore black and white or black and purple—"half-mourning" it was called.

Now responsibilities began in earnest. The older girls were married, and Nellie, despite the fact that she was only twelve, became mistress of the home, looked after household tasks, and presided at the table. She had not gone to school since leaving Oberlin but had devoted herself to learning housekeeping. Mr. Spencer had hired a woman to teach Nellie to cook, to prepare vegetables and meats, to bake cakes, pies, and salt-rising bread, and to sew patchwork. She took lessons on the melodeon, too. She began to feel that she was a young lady.

But she did not dress as a young lady. Her skirts were still short. Secretly, however, she longed to let them down for there were often young men students about the Spencer home and Nellie had noted that the young ladies who wore long dresses received the most attention. She visioned herself in long skirts. Opportunity to wear them soon came.

Mr. Spencer had many calls for teachers of penmanship, but during the war it was sometimes difficult to supply this demand and, when a request came from North Kingsville, Ohio, there was not a teacher available. Thereupon Mr. Spencer decided to send twelve-year-old Nellie. She must, of course, look mature and dignified now. She must wear long dresses. Joyfully, she let out tucks and hems.

Her father arranged for her to stay with friends in North Kingsville, wrote all the copies for her to use in the penmanship course, gave her minute instructions, and Nellie set forth, the youngest teacher in Ohio, Mr. Spencer declared proudly.

The penmanship classes were held in the evening at the schoolhouse, and the students were adults, men and women earning their own living, so that the matter of discipline was negligible. But one evening Nellie found the classroom in an uproar. Some one had written a bit of foolishness on the blackboard and the class was screaming with laughter.

Nellie tried to be dignified. She asked that the person responsible for the writing come up and erase it. But no one came, and the hilarity merely increased. Nellie was at a loss what to do. Then it occurred to her that these people had asked for a teacher, were paying their own money to be taught penmanship. With all the firmness she could muster, she told them the class would not proceed until the guilty person should erase the remark from the blackboard.

The room suddenly became silent. After a bit, a man got up, said he guessed he might as well do it first as last, and striding to the blackboard he removed the distracting statement. He was a burly fellow, a railroad worker. Nellie was amazed at her victory.

After this teaching experience she went with her father

to Ashtabula to give a course in penmanship. They stayed at the hotel, and to Nellie this seemed very grand and important. And, since Mr. Spencer knew a great many people in Ashtabula, he and Nellie were entertained frequently. There were attentive young men about, too. Nellie was all aflutter with the excitement of living.

But it was high time to attend to the sober business of getting an education, and in the spring she became a student at Geneva High School. This scholastic venture, however, was brief. She had to stay in town except for week-ends and without her it became lonely at the farm. Mr. Spencer could not bear the loneliness, and Nellie had to come home again. But she was not to be denied an education and her father engaged his niece, Mrs. Sarah Hayden, to teach Nellie at home and prepare her for work later at a seminary. Mrs. Hayden also taught little Emma; her own son, Maitland, and Louise Morrison, daughter of a neighboring family, Barzillai and Minerva Morrison.

Staying at home suited Nellie perfectly. She studied, looked after the household tasks, and attended to the comforts of the boys who were in the army, sent them pies, cakes, and jellies. She was quite domestic. Housekeeping was difficult, too, because of the war. Everything was high-priced and often necessities could not be had at all. The cost of sugar was prohibitive and sorghum, bitter and ill-tasting, was used as a substitute.

Cotton goods were very scarce. When sheets wore out they had to be patched, repatched, and pieced together in a most astonishing manner. When women wanted new calico dresses they had to scour all the stores of the countryside for material. One day word passed about that a merchant at Unionville, eight miles away, had received a large lot of calico remnants, and Nellie with the neighborhood women hurried to make purchases. Dresses that resulted were riotous in color, for calico was printed in brilliant reds, yellows, blues, and purples, and it took many remnants to supply the yardage required by fashions in the sixties.

There were always merry times at the Spencer home

when any of the boys came home on a furlough. In the evening after supper the young folks drove to town to get the mail and on the way home they usually sang, particularly if it was a moonlight night. Such songs as "John Brown's Body" and "Tramp, Tramp, Tramp, the Boys Are Marching" were popular.

A serious problem of the war was the care of sick and injured soldiers, for there was no Red Cross at this time. But its forerunner, the United States Sanitary Commission, had been organized for soldier relief, chiefly through the efforts of Dr. Elizabeth Blackwell, first woman to receive the degree of M.D. in the United States; and to raise money for the Commission, fairs were held in various cities. Nellie Spencer attended one of these fairs held in Cleveland, Ohio.

It was a memorable event. For the first time in her life, she heard a speech by a woman, Miss Anna E. Dickinson, noted orator of the time. Nellie was thrilled. She marveled that a woman could speak so well. And for that matter so did everybody else. In fact, so brilliant were Miss Dickinson's speeches, certain folk contended that a man must have written them.

Though Nellie greatly admired Miss Dickinson it did not occur to her to try to follow in Miss Dickinson's footsteps. The latter was too unusual, too different from the women of the everyday world, the women of Nellie's world. But she thought a great deal about Miss Dickinson and was impressed by her lovely personal appearance, especially by the fact that her hair was cut short, a popular feminine fashion—a style that Mr. Spencer hotly opposed, and Nellie had to promise him never to cut her hair. But she complied readily. It was seldom that she did anything to displease her father. But one day he was very severe with her.

Neighborhood girls came to visit Nellie, and she took them horseback riding. Mr. Spencer was fond of horses and he had several of an unusual breed, dark blue-gray in color, called the "blue" horses. One of them, "Old Charley," had been in the family for years, and Old Charley was somewhat of a misogynist. When a woman came near him his ears lay back and his eyes gleamed maliciously. But he sometimes allowed Nellie privileges and since there were not enough other horses on this day, she mounted Old Charley. And he seemed docile enough.

When the young ladies were returning from their ride, however, Old Charley suddenly stopped by a ditch, arched his back, and deposited Nellie in a puddle. Then he turned and looked at her as if to say in his own horse way that he didn't want to hurt her but he had had quite enough of this woman foolishness.

A hired man reported the incident to Mr. Spencer and, though Nellie was uninjured, her father reproved her sternly and forbade her ever going horseback riding again. It never occurred to her to disobey him.

Early in 1864 Mr. Spencer was called to New York City to confer with publishers and give courses in penmanship and he left Nellie, who was now nearly fourteen years of age, in full charge of the management of the farm. Among other things she must attend to the selling of a thousand bushels of corn. It was of excellent quality and she was determined to get the top price.

But buyers came, inspected the corn, and made offers considerably below her expectations. She refused to sell. Others came and still the offers were low.

Nellie began to worry. She was afraid she might not sell the corn at all if she insisted upon the highest price. She went to a neighbor, Mr. Jacquays, for advice. She had known him from babyhood, for Mr. Jacquays had been a frequent visitor at the Spencer home. He reassured her about the corn and told her to hold it.

Not long afterward a buyer came, offered the top price, and paid Nellie in cash. That was a great day in her life. She fairly burst with pride and happiness and her father, when he heard the news, was lavish with praise.

He kept in close touch with the activities of the farm and wrote often to Nellie and Emma. In one letter he described New York.

Platt R. Spencer

Feb. 6, 1864

My dear Daughters Nellie and Emma—

I am thinking of you tonight, my darlings, and all the household and the dear old home with all its comforts. I can hardly contain myself such is my strong desire to be with you.

No school at the College today, no writing class this evening. I have been writing most of the day diligently but this afternoon took a walk down Broadway about 2½ miles. . . .

Broadway is the most thronged and fashionable thoroughfare in the city—the sidewalks alive with well dressed pedestrians of both sexes—the streets crowded with gaudy carriages filled with the same flaunting material. One current on each sidewalk is setting north and another south and the same in the streets—thus six of horses, carriages, and human beings are in constant motion and frequently (especially at the crossing of other streets) so crowded and huddled that all have to halt and disentangle.

The houses, stores, and buildings are from four to six stories high, with glass doors and a wilderness of display of every conceivable article of merchandise, for nearly four miles. I wish I could pilot my daughters down this street once and watch the roll of the eye endeavoring to drink in so many things at once.

I arrived at my room precisely at supper time, six o'clock. Have been out since and bought a lamp, funnel, and shade, with can and oil, also candles, etc., and now for the first time since I came to the city have a good light to write by.

A large manufacturing establishment is now burning a few blocks below here but the Yorkers are so used to fires, they make little fuss about it. Henry is at the theatre tonight, he urged me to go but I felt I had rather write to the dear ones at home. My task is pretty hard teaching at the college—the morning class from nine to ten numbers about eighty and the evening class from seven to nine about sixty—and I have to write all the copies. My correspondence follows me and is accumulating on my hands.

. . . Well now I must close and soon retire. Oh! what would I give to have my head combed tonight and warm my feet by the good large fire in the sitting room.

When you write please say something of what A——— is doing and if you need money. Give my love to all.

Your aff. Father
P. R. Spencer

Have scratched this letter rather rapidly—please excuse.

Father.

Mr. Spencer returned from New York a worn, ill man. He had taken a severe cold and had been unable to throw it off. The family was shocked and frightened at his condition, but he would not admit he was sick, would not give up and remain in bed. A serious lung trouble developed. Physicians were called in consultation from Cleveland but to no avail. Mr. Spencer died May 16, 1864, three days after Nellie's fourteenth birthday.

It seemed the very end of her world. For her father had been her teacher, her confidant, her ally. And now that he was gone the home would be broken up, the old and happy order of living changed.

Educational circles mourned Platt Spencer's death. Business colleges throughout the country draped his portrait in black, and people thronged to his funeral. Nellie would never forget the endless line of carriages and buggies that followed his body to the Evergreen Cemetery in Geneva. Nor would she forget the tributes to her father's work. "He was a great man," they said. "He taught America to write."

CHAPTER III

STRANGE OPPORTUNITY

Fatherless as well as motherless now, Nellie and her little sister, Emma, must depend upon their older brothers and sisters. Nellie went to Milwaukee to make her home with her brother, Robert, and his wife, while Emma went to Chicago to stay with Sara and her husband, Junius R. Sloan, an artist. To the brothers and sisters this seemed the best plan, but for the two girls it was a most unhappy arrangement. Because of the separation, the strangeness and dreariness of the new life, Nellie was desperately lonely and homesick.

She must wear full mourning, too, the family decided. She was quite old enough, they thought. But the gloomy black with its somber crepe veil depressed her and kept her always conscious of her sorrow. And at times it made her uncomfortably conspicuous.

Nellie had flaming red cheeks, and the wearing of black accentuated her coloring. Often she was accused of painting, an odious imputation, for nice women did not paint. Sometimes men stared at her rudely and once when she was visiting Sara and they were out walking, the latter noticed this and directed Nellie to draw her veil over her face. Life seemed filled with distress. The strain of it told upon Nellie's health.

And little Emma in the midst of these readjustments was stricken with a severe illness. Within a few months after Mr. Spencer's death, she, too, was taken, and once again the family gathered at Geneva for a funeral. Nellie, through shock and grief, collapsed at the farm home. She was ill for a long time.

She was at home, however, among familiar scenes, and her sister, Phoebe—Mrs. Adams—remained to care for her. There were old friends and neighbors about, too, and the family physician, Dr. Edson, called daily. Slowly Nellie's strength returned.

That winter she went to Poughkeepsie, N. Y., to be with her brother, Henry, who had recently married and was teaching penmanship at the Bryant and Stratton Business College. Henry and his wife, Sally, lived at a hotel overlooking the Hudson River, and winter sports were in full swing with ice-boating, skating, and sleighing. Nellie, watching these gay activities from her window, began to feel a returning zest in life.

One afternoon she herself went sleighing with Henry and Sally to the outskirts of Poughkeepsie to see what was considered a most preposterous undertaking, Vassar College, founded in 1861, the first school in the world designed to give a full collegiate education to women. It had aroused widespread curiosity, and people were discussing with amazement the imposing new college building with more than two hundred rooms and accommodations for four hundred students. Surely, people declared, in the whole country there could not be as many as four hundred young women who would want a higher education.

Matthew Vassar, founder of the college, was a wealthy brewer and was generally conceded to be a capable business man, but heads wagged ominously over this college venture.

The Vassars were Baptists, and at church Nellie made the acquaintance of Matthew Vassar, Jr., nephew of the elder Vassar. He wanted her to enroll as a student at the college and was quite willing to make allowances in regard to scholastic requirements, but neither Nellie or her brother thought a college education necessary or even advisable. Besides, Nellie was hardly well enough to think of going to school.

To build up her strength she went with Sally to New York to take the water-cure, a treatment including baths, packs, and special diets, very much in vogue for physical ailments.

New York was celebrating Lee's surrender. Streets and buildings were gay with flags and the populace was in a veritable paroxysm of joy. Then, with shocking suddenness, triumphant gaiety changed to grief and bitterness while bright bunting was displaced by black draperies. Lincoln had been assassinated.

His funeral train came to New York. His body lay in state in the City Hall, and throughout the day and night thousands filed by his bier to pay their respects. Nellie and Sally went at midnight to avoid the vast crowds.

It was a hushed hour with dim lights, and Lincoln lay stark and pale in his great coffin while the ghostly shadows of people moved softly about. Young Nellie was intensely awed.

Besides its Vassar College for higher learning, Poughkeepsie had several seminaries for young ladies. The town also boasted two business colleges, and hundreds of young men, marching home from the war, enrolled at the business colleges. The town was filled with youth in spirited eager hosts. The tension of the war was ended, and it was spring. Poughkeepsie saw merry stirring times.

The seminaries, to be sure, were very strict with their young ladies, but the young ladies managed to have good times in spite of that. They found innumerable excuses for going out walking. And there were the young men out walking, too. Getting acquainted became most informal, youthful flirtations quite the fashion. One young "flapper" devised an unique way of making acquaintances. She wore a ribbon on her shoulder and when she saw a young man whom she liked, she dropped the ribbon so that he could pick it up. Then he might walk with her.

Nellie at this time got a job in the office of the Bryant and Stratton Business College and she met many young people. She learned to dance and she went to parties. And she fell in love. But she had no intention of getting married. Of course she planned to marry sometime. She thought it was the duty of every woman to marry and have children, but that obligation she consigned to the very, very distant future. Much more interesting things were to be done now.

Calisthenics were becoming popular, and Nellie with others joined a gymnasium class to play games and take exercises to promote health and grace. Then she became a student at Rice's Young Ladies' Seminary where she planned to finish her schooling. But this venture like the former ones came to an abrupt end. Henry and Sally decided to go to Ohio, and Nellie went with them.

Later she enrolled at the Lake Erie Seminary, Painesville, Ohio. But soon illness intervened and once again she gave up school. Life was very impermanent, a constant moving from one thing to another and from this place to that.

After a while she went to South Bend, Indiana, to stay with her sister, Phoebe, whose husband, Mr. Adams, conducted a business college. At this time the great majority of students at all business colleges were young men but there were a few young women and Nellie enrolled for a business course.

She found a most absorbing subject, business law. And she revealed such a remarkable aptitude for it that, in spite of the fact that she was but sixteen and a girl, the only girl in a class of nineteen, the instructor, who was an attorney and mayor of South Bend, called her aside one day and asked her to go into his office and seriously take up the study of law.

Nellie was dumfounded. Never in all her life had she heard anything so amazing, so utterly absurd as this and she could only gasp, "There are no women lawyers."

"Not yet," he admitted, "but there will be women lawyers and you will be one."

But Nellie could not believe anything so obviously ridiculous. Lawyers were always men. No women were admitted to the bar. Therefore the law was a man's job, not woman's, and Nellie would most assuredly not think of undertaking it.

Yet the law did seem a most fascinating profession. She wished that she were a man.

Then the whole incident was forgotten. Phoebe, long in ill health, died, and Nellie, once again plunged in sorrow, went to Milwaukee to her brother, Robert.

Robert Spencer conducted a business college and had won a reputation as an educator. He wanted Nellie to finish school and at this time arranged for her to become a student-teacher at Rockford Seminary, Rockford, Illinois. She taught penmanship and calisthenics and studied Latin, English, and literature. One of her teachers, a friend of Robert, was Miss Charlotte Emerson, a relative of Ralph Waldo Emerson.

Rockford Seminary was non-sectarian but strict in religious observance, and the spiritual welfare of the students was the chief concern of the Principal, Miss S———, an intensely devout woman. Miss S—— liked to have her students go into religious work and nothing pleased her more than to have one of her girls marry a minister, preferably one going into the mission field. She was inclined to take a hand in making such matches and often invited eligible young clergymen to her school to meet the more serious-minded young ladies.

Sometimes the matchmaking did not progress to her liking and then Miss S——— was apt to have a conference with the young lady in question. Interviews of this nature were a source of much speculation among the other students, particularly if the young lady emerged red-eyed and miserable.

But Miss S——— made no effort to marry Nellie Spencer to a minister. Perhaps it was because Nellie was not as spiritually-minded as Miss S——— wished. Indeed Nellie found it extremely difficult to comply with all the religious demands of Rockford. One of them was the prayer service held daily just before midday dinner, with small groups of young women meeting in the rooms of faculty members.

Nellie met with the group in Miss S———'s office and with the other young women was expected to take her turn daily in prayer. But Nellie was sensitive and shy, she had never prayed in public, and days passed without her taking part vocally in the prayer service.

Usually prayers ended with the sounding of the dinner gong, Miss S——— rising and the young ladies following, but one day when the bell rang, Miss S——— remained kneeling. Questioning glances escaped from the lowered eyes of the young women in the circle but none of them dared rise until the Principal did. Yet all of them had prayed except Nellie Spencer. The silence became intense.

Outside in the hall, other students were hurrying to the dining room. Still Miss S——— kept her young ladies kneeling. Nellie was painfully aware that she was being disciplined and if she did not pray the other girls in the group might have to go dinnerless. Miserably, falteringly, Nellie prayed. At once Miss S——— arose and dismissed the young ladies.

Rockford rules were exacting. Students must get up at a certain time, go to bed at a certain time, get permission before going anywhere, and always be properly chaperoned even when they went to church. But young ladies occasionally broke the rules and defiantly stole out by way of a window or unguarded rear door to meet the young men of the town. This was a grave misdemeanor and, if discovered, was likely to be punished by suspension. And if a young lady transgressed a second time, she was apt to be expelled.

For the infraction of minor rules, young ladies were punished by being put on probation and sent to room with a faculty member. Usually, the girls resented this discipline, but one young woman, sent to room with the new student-teacher, Nellie Spencer, seemed pleased, even eager at the prospect. Nellie soon learned the reason.

Rockford had no running water and no bath rooms but each room was equipped with a wash bowl and pitcher filled with water from a cistern in the yard. And the first time Nellie washed her face after the arrival of her charge, the latter was a vitally interested spectator.

As Nellie finished, the girl exclaimed, "Why, you don't paint your cheeks, do you?" The students, she said, had taken sides as to whether Miss Spencer's complexion was natural or artificial, and the young lady under discipline had been delegated to settle the question.

Frivolities were frowned upon at Rockford and such light-minded pastimes as cards and dancing were taboo. But the forbidden things became all the more alluring and even Nellie, usually so shy and compliant, was moved to a bit of deviltry. In charge of a literary society entertainment, one of Rockford's important events to which the townspeople were invited, Nellie as teacher of calisthenics bethought herself of a way to add variety to the usual recitations and musical selections. She would have some dancing.

It was likely, she told herself naughtily, that the pious Miss S——— had never seen any dancing and would not recognize it. And of course it would not be called dancing. The young ladies in gymnasium costume would simply be doing graceful exercises. But the students knew they were practicing nothing more or less than a square dance and the audacity of it inspired them. Rehearsals went ahead with enthusiasm.

The evening of the entertainment found the young women perfect in their performance, but Nellie by this time was exceedingly nervous. Suppose Miss S——— should suspect. . . . All during the "dance" number Nellie watched the Principal's face to note her reaction. But that good lady, as the students moved gracefully about the floor, nodded a dignified approval and when the dance ended and the spectators broke into a storm of applause, Miss S——— was actually beaming. Whether she ever knew that a dance had been perpetrated under her very nose, Nellie did not learn. Miss S——— never mentioned the subject.

But Nellie paid. She had given herself so completely to the excitement and labor of preparation for the entertainment that she overtaxed her strength and once again she became ill. Miss Emerson took care of her and Nellie improved slightly but she could not go on with her work, and Robert came to take her home.

When he arrived Miss S——— asked him to give a talk to the young ladies. He warned the Principal that he might speak of something which she did not approve but, sure that he would do no such thing, she still urged him to speak and he took part in the morning chapel exercises.

His subject was a New York newspaper which was banned at Rockford because it contained detective stories and sensational news items. And to Miss S———'s horror, Spencer urged the young women to read this paper. He explained that a noted divine, Henry Ward Beecher, was writing articles for the publication, and of course Miss S——— could not question the propriety of reading Mr. Beecher's writings.

After a summer vacation in Milwaukee, Nellie returned to Rockford but her energies seemed unequal to the task, and shortly afterward she took final leave of Rockford. She went now to make her home with her sister, Sara, who had moved to Yonkers, N. Y.

Nellie's brother, Henry, and his wife, Sally, were in Washington, D. C., where Henry was teaching penmanship at the Spencerian Business College, a school, like many others, named for Platt Spencer. By this time more young women were seeking a business education, and this college had organized a ladies' department. A woman was needed to take charge of it, and Henry suggested Nellie for the place. It seemed befitting that a Spencerian Business College should have two Spencers on its faculty, and the principal gladly offered Nellie the job.

She accepted with alacrity for Sally had been writing glowing accounts of Washington, the White House, the Capitol, and the gay social life.

Chapter IV

WASHINGTON, D. C., 1869

As the Baltimore and Ohio train on which she was riding neared the District of Columbia one sultry morning early in September, 1869, Nellie Spencer, all agog for a glimpse of her new world, sighted the Capitol building, its great dome etched in gleaming splendor against the sky. It was symbolic. It was Washington. Never in all her nineteen years had she been so thrilled.

With a hundred eager questions she turned to her brother, Henry, who was accompanying her from New York, but Henry remained engrossed in a book. That anyone could read amidst the excitement of approaching the national capital was wholly beyond Nellie. She could hardly contain herself.

Presently the train stopped at the small B. and O. station where hackney cabs, many of them in a most dilapidated condition, waited to convey the people about the city, the drivers in sharp competition for patronage. But Nellie and her brother boarded a horse car, a squat vehicle that swayed rollickingly as it moved and had such high seats that Nellie's feet did not reach the floor.

Numerous complaints were made about the horse cars, particularly in winter, for they were unheated and were held blamable for many Washingtonian colds and attacks of rheumatism. It was often suggested that stoves, such as were used on the steam railways, be installed in the horse cars, but they were not forthcoming. "A stove," scoffed the irate passengers, "might occupy the space of three or four 'fares'." But the street car company did make some effort to provide relief from cold. The floors of the cars were covered with straw to protect the passengers' feet.

Henry and Sally Spencer lived on Fifth Street, Northwest, just off what was often spoken of as fashionable M Street, and here Nellie settled down, aglow with anticipation.

Yet Washington in 1869 was far from being a place of beauty. Despite its population of more than one hundred thousand, it was little more than an overgrown village, straggling and unkempt, with fashionable homes and tumble-down shanties hobnobbing unrestrictedly in every section and streets that billowed with dust in dry weather and were a vast network of bogs in wet weather.

Sanitary conditions were deplorable. The Federal city had been established amidst swamps and swamps still abounded. Toward the west along the Potomac River was a marshy region known as Foggy Bottom; in the northeast, beyond the Capitol, was a vast stretch of swamps called Swampoodle; along the eastern branch, later known as the Anacostia River, was more low, wet land; to the south, the Mall was a morass, turned into a lake when the spring rains fell; what later was to become Potomac Park was a region of mud, water, and underbrush; and close to the White House, itself, was a great pond. The city was a veritable paradise for mosquitoes, and epidemics of malaria were frequent and virulent.

Methods of sewage disposal were primitive. A few short stretches of sewers had been built but, for the most part, the numerous streams of the District were used for this purpose. The old Washington Canal, long in disuse, had been turned into a noisome sewer, and Tiber Creek, near the Capitol, was the chief sewer of that community. Wells furnished most of the drinking water and everywhere were privies, the removal of night soil filling the city with a great stench. But health authorities were recommending ways and means of deodorization.

Garbage was piled in hillocks along the streets and alleys, and cows, hogs, and geese, roaming at large, scattered this refuse as they foraged. Such animals were a constant nuisance, especially the hogs, and one angry citizen in the west-end wrote to the *Evening Star* to complain of conditions in his neighborhood and to ask why the hog catcher did not do his duty.

"Hogs roam streets, alleys, and avenues, day and night, week-days and Sundays without fear," he lamented. "They dispute possession of the sidewalk with pedestrians. They insinuate their swinish snouts into all private passages and all gates left ajar. They bring devastation and ruin to gardens and ornamental grounds." He added that they made "unseemly skirmish in the streets with dogs and schoolboys and seemed to be on the best terms with the police who are never known to interfere with their enjoyment of the largest liberty."

The police, however, had other and more serious tasks than hog catching. Lawlessness was rampant in such sections as Bloodfield, Bloody Hill, and Hell's Bottom, the latter notorious for its gangs, its brawls, and murders. The city, too, was glutted with saloons, many of them most disreputable in character. And night provided a cloak of darkness for the perpetration of crime, for streets had but a few dim lights and alleys were entirely without illumination.

But here and there the District of Columbia revealed evidence of national pride and development. It had broad streets and avenues, planned to give beautiful vistas; it had the White House, stately and palatial; the Treasury Building; the Smithsonian Institution; the Patent Office; and the Capitol had been given a fine new dome and two new wings. There were a few parks, too: Lafayette Square, opposite the White House; Franklin Park; Judiciary Square, and the Botanical Gardens. But public grounds were generally unimproved. Memorials were few, but work had been started on the Washington Monument and, like a huge factory chimney, it towered above the swampy Mall, amidst shacks and broken stones.

Very little street paving had been done and some of that could not be pointed to with pride. The principal thoroughfare, Pennsylvania Avenue, planned to be an impressive connecting link between the White House and the Capitol, one and a third miles distant, was laid with cobble stones and so rough that riding over it wrought havoc to both spines and dispositions.

The city's main business section centered about the north side of Pennsylvania Avenue, Seventh Street, and D Street but stores had not developed along the south side of the Avenue, its extreme width proving somewhat of a barrier to shoppers. Certain pursuits, however, had taken root there. Flaunting itself almost within the very shadow of the White House and extending eastward toward the Capitol was Washington's notorious red-light section.

Nice women dared not walk along this side of the Avenue. Venturesome ones when irreproachably escorted, occasionally did cross the Avenue at Eleventh to Harvey's Restaurant, a popular eating place, but many women, mindful of a fair name, would take no such risk as that. Nice men, though, were not troubled by these limitations.

This section had fallen into disrepute during the Civil War when Gen. Hooker's Division had camped there and the usual camp followers had come to prey upon the regiments. After the war the soldiers had disbanded but the flotsam and jetsam remained, and this section, dubbed "The Division," continued its activity for nearly fifty years before Congress took action to remove it.

Improvements were slow in coming to Washington. In fact so little was done that many plans were being discussed for moving the capital elsewhere, St. Louis being often mentioned as a more suitable location. People argued that this was the only course open toward establishing a capital worthy of the nation. They were certain Washington could never be developed into a beautiful city.

But Nellie Spencer found no fault with it. The President lived there; Congress met there; it was the gathering place of important people; its social life was delightful; indeed it seemed a most alluring place. She wanted to see everything at once. As principal of the ladies' department of the Spencerian Business College, however, she must attend to duty first.

This department had been formed to meet a demand. Women were being taken into government service and they needed training. The first woman to be employed by a government department had been Miss Clara Barton who, in 1854, through a relative in Congress, had been appointed head clerk in the Patent Office. Later, in 1862, Gen. Francis E. Spinner, Treasurer of the U. S., employed women to cut Treasury notes because, as he said, "A woman can use shears better than a man and she will do it cheaper."

Since then many women left in want by the war had come to Washington to seek jobs. They were doing a variety of government work and they attended evening classes at the business college to study such subjects as bookkeeping and penmanship, the latter most important, for there were no typewriters and all letters and documents had to be written in long hand.

The ladies' department held day classes, too, for young girls who had completed the eighth grade and who did not care to attend any of the city's numerous finishing schools.

Washington had no high schools. Though high schools were common in New England and the middle west, Washington officials would countenance no spending of public money for such an extravagance. Nor was there a Normal School. Even the grade schools were poorly organized and were often referred to as pauper schools because they were free. Some improvements were being made in the school system, however, and Franklin School was dedicated that fall. It would accommodate as many as nine hundred children and was considered one of the finest school buildings in the country.

At the business college Nellie Spencer became at once Miss Nellie to students and teachers, and this informality charmed her. She found the president of the school, Mr. H. N. Copp, very agreeable, too, and it was he who accompanied her on her first visit to the Capitol. They visited the United States Supreme Court which was in session with the Chief Justice, Salmon P. Chase, presiding, a solemn and awe-inspiring meeting. Nellie could hardly believe she was actually there witnessing it. She felt strangely exalted.

And had anyone dared to suggest that she herself might one day argue cases before this most supreme tribunal, she would have thought the speaker suddenly bereft of his senses. People in general would have laughed outright at the supposition of a woman being admitted to practice before any court, much less the United States Supreme Court. But that same year, 1869, a woman, Mrs. Arabella A. Mansfield, was formally admitted to the bar in Iowa, the first of her sex to achieve that distinction in this country. And elsewhere other women were struggling for this same recognition.

But Nellie Spencer had not heard of them. She was too absorbed in her own immediate world. She was seeing Washington.

On her first Saturday afternoon in the city she attended a Marine Band concert given in the White House grounds. These were held every Saturday afternoon during the summer and fall when the weather permitted and were popular occasions. Between numbers, people strolled about to greet friends and to take note of the fashions in dress. Ladies were wearing stiffly starched dresses with overskirts and carried small ruffled parasols to protect their complexions from the sun.

Then came a reception at the White House. Several were held each winter and Washingtonians flocked to the Executive Mansion. Nellie was all aflutter at the thought of actually meeting the President, Ulysses S. Grant, and Mrs. Grant, and for this momentous occasion Nellie and Sally put on their smartest dresses, black silk grosgrain with trains, the trains being detachable and fastened to a band about the waist.

The two young women were accompanied by Henry and a young man acquaintance, and upon their arrival at the White House, were admitted at the front door and their wraps taken by maids in a room at the right. Hats and coats were piled in heaps on boxes and benches with no system whatever for identification, thus causing considerable confusion and delay when it came time to go home. But this was accepted as a natural part of a White House reception.

Guests were hurried into line in the main hall and rushed through the Red parlor and the Green parlor to the Blue room, where President and Mrs. Grant were receiving. Nellie was too excited to take note of the furnishings as she passed for she was staring ahead for a glimpse of the host and hostess. Then, incredible as it seemed, she was standing before them, was being introduced by a military aide and was being greeted in a decidedly pleasant and friendly manner. It was immensely satisfying.

Mrs. Grant was not as pretty as Nellie would have liked but the First Lady was so cordial that Nellie loved her at once. Mrs. Grant's eyes were crossed and the story was told that a surgeon offered to perform an operation to remedy this defect but Mr. Grant declined, saying he had always known her as she was and loved her that way. Mrs. Grant, it seemed, had been quite willing to abide by this decision.

As soon as the guests had paid their respects to the President and Mrs. Grant, they gathered in the great east room where they visited with each other as much as was possible amidst the jostling, scrambling crowds that always attended a public reception.

Receptions were rife in Washington. Newspapers announced, "The receptions of the Speaker of the House of Representatives, James G. Blaine, will be held at his residence, 408 Fifteenth Street, from 9 to 11 o'clock on each Friday evening of the season. Mrs. Blaine's receptions will be held every Wednesday of the season between the hours of 2 and 5, p. m.

"At the Russian Legation, Madame de Catacazy will receive on Thursdays from 2 to 5, p. m. At the Argentine Legation, Madame de Garcia will receive on alternate Monday evenings.

"The next levee of President Grant will be given on Thursday, the 24th inst., between the hours of 8 and 10, p. m. Mrs. Grant's receptions will be held every Tuesday during the season between the hours of 2 and 4, p. m."

Social life was very democratic and opportunities to meet people of fame and importance were numerous. When

Prince Arthur, son of Queen Victoria, visited Washington that winter, nearly everyone, especially the young ladies, looked forward to making his acquaintance. Of course he was entertained at select functions but he was a guest, too, at more informal parties.

He attended a public reception at the home of Speaker Blaine. Nellie Spencer with a group of young women learned that the Prince was to be at the Blaine home and hurried there in great excitement to make his acquaintance. Nellie had not yet met Mr. Blaine and when she was introduced to him he asked if she was the daughter of Senator Spencer.

"No, indeed!" Nellie replied quickly, for she had heard much disapproval of certain of Senator Spencer's political activities. "I am the daughter of Platt R. Spencer," she asserted proudly.

Then came the coveted meeting with the Prince. Slim and young, he appeared very handsome to most of the young ladies, but to Nellie he was a great disappointment. He seemed so immature, so unimposing for a Prince. She left the reception, fully convinced that American men were very much better looking than Englishmen, and this conclusion gave her a great deal of satisfaction.

Among Washington's gayest and most joyfully anticipated social events were the New Year receptions. Practically everyone, the President, cabinet members, senators, representatives, city officials, and non-officials, kept open house, the ladies remaining at home or joining other women to receive while the men made the calls. But at the White House it was stated specifically that "ladies will be received."

Most homes served refreshments with plenty of liquor for all who might come, because it was hardly thought to be a holiday without considerable drinking and carousing. The times, however, were becoming less tempestuous for the *Evening Star* commented that Christmas of 1869 saw "much less drinking, gambling, shooting, disorder, and noise" than was usual at holiday time. A movement was afoot, too, to make the New Year celebrations more quiet and temperate and a few officials agreed to dispense with intoxicating liquors and serve coffee and chocolate instead, with plenty of cake and sandwiches. But liquor was rather generally served and drunken and tipsy men were a common sight in the streets.

Among homes of congressmen open for the New Year was that of Gen. and Mrs. James A. Garfield, who had just built a house at the corner of Thirteenth and Eye Streets, N. W. They were close friends of the Spencers and a part of the time while waiting for their new home to be finished, had resided with Henry and Sally Spencer.

Young Nellie fairly worshiped Garfield. A large man, tall, sandy-haired, and bearded, she thought him very handsome. Also he was a member of that most fascinating profession, the law. They often had long talks together, usually about politics or religion, and sometimes Garfield spoke of his political aspirations. He was ambitious to become President but was doubtful of ever achieving that goal. He was a great admirer of Lincoln and one day he told Nellie that he thought Lincoln had died most gloriously, that he himself could ask nothing greater than to die as Lincoln had. She was to recall that remark vividly, years later, when Garfield had become President.

The Garfields were not wealthy and Lucretia Garfield, limited as to funds, had been considerably worried about providing curtains for her new home in time for the New Year reception, but she solved the problem by purchasing white muslin and making the curtains, herself.

Nellie celebrated the New Year at the Business College where she and the young ladies received the young men from twelve to six and passed the evening in dancing.

As principal of the ladies' department of a business college, Nellie Spencer was a person of some consequence, and when the women suffragists held their second annual convention in Washington that winter, they sought her support. Her sister-in-law, Sally, was an ardent suffragist and a friend of Phoebe Couzins, active in the feminist movement, and through them Nellie made the acquaintance of Susan B. Anthony, Elizabeth Cady Stanton, Matilda Joslyn Gage, Lucretia Mott, and others.

They took Nellie with them to sit on the platform. A fearful ordeal for her because woman suffrage was most unpopular, suffragists were ridiculed and scorned and Nellie, though she was not to speak, was not to take any active part whatever in the program, was so terrified that she trembled from head to foot. Lucretia Mott, noting this, said, "Thee is frightened." And Nellie admitted that she was.

Miss Anthony, wearing, as usual, a black silk dress with a red-fringed shawl about her shoulders, presided, faced the crowd coolly, demanded the rights of suffrage amidst jeers, and answered the hecklers with a sparkling wit. She was an amazing woman and a gifted woman, and Nellie admired her at once.

But Nellie knew she could never do what Miss Anthony was doing. The very thought of speaking before a crowd, even a friendly one, filled Nellie with dread. She believed women should have the right to vote and remembered that her father had signed suffrage petitions and had said his daughter would need the vote more than her brothers, still she had no inclination to become a crusader for the cause. It seemed too hopeless. And life was already filled with so many pleasant things. Gaily, Nellie followed the more comfortable pathway.

Spring came and brought long rides about the city and country bursting forth in all its new green glory. Livery stables were numerous with fine horses and gay equipages. Harness gleamed with metal mountings and victorias were the height of fashion.

Holidays always meant a thriving business for the livery stables and on May 30, 1870, the third annual celebration of Memorial Day, the populace rushed to get carriages to go to Arlington for the program, a speech by Gen. Logan, music by the Marine Band, and a grand chorus of five hundred voices.

According to the *Evening Star* "at least twenty thousand persons were present although the roads leading to Arlington were in a terrible condition and in many instances the horses were unable to draw their loads through the mud until relieved of some of the weight."

Livery stables did such a large business that a "conveyance could not be had at any price after twelve o'clock. The tariff for the day was from $15 to $20 for a horse and buggy though it was probably well worth that price on account of the roads, which had a fearful effect on horse flesh."

Refreshment stands were not allowed inside the cemetery but "venders of cakes, pies, and fruits, 'cool lager' and sparkling lemonade" held forth all along the route from the aqueduct bridge to Arlington and proprietors "in loud terms praised the quality of their beverages and eatables."

Many Washingtonians liked to visit Arlington the day after the ceremonies to see the flowers, and Nellie accompanied by the young man of the moment went on that day to the cemetery. They rode in a victoria drawn by a dashing, ornately harnessed team of horses.

In June commencement exercises were held at the Spencerian Business College and Nellie was very proud of her seven young women graduates. But there were many more young men to graduate and since both sexes were represented it was thought best to have two commencement speakers. Grace Greenwood, writer and lecturer, spoke for the young ladies and General John Eaton, Commissioner of Education, for the young men.

Directly afterward Nellie left Washington to stay for the summer with her sister, Sara. No one who could possibly avoid it remained in Washington through July and August because the heat was intense, mosquitoes a constant pest, and outbreaks of malaria frequent. Sometimes as early as May the press would warn the populace that the "mosquitoes are sharpening their bills."

When the wind was from the east or south from over the vast mosquito-breeding territories it was highly uncomfortable and even dangerous to sit outside in the evening but if the wind was from the north or west, residents might with safety and pleasure enjoy their porches and gardens.

Malaria was the scourge of White House families, and a summer cottage was maintained for the President at the Soldiers' Home on the highlands north of the city. Lincoln had stayed there through the hot weather and other Presidents found it a desirable retreat.

Chapter V

MARRIAGE

Henry and Sally Spencer were attending the Church of the New Jerusalem, founded on the writings of Emmanuel Swedenborg, and they were doing a great deal of reading regarding its teachings. Nellie at once became interested, went to the church services, and was a guest at the social gatherings. She loved parties.

One of these church parties became a never-to-be-forgotten milestone in her life. Faintly but unmistakably it marked the beginning of events that were to color and shape her destiny, to carve out the pattern of her ability, now so hopelessly embedded in traditions.

Often the church "sociables" included programs of music and literature, and at one of them, held in December, 1869, General Reuben Delavan Mussey was a speaker. A commanding figure more than six feet in height was General Mussey with a leonine head, a mass of gold red hair, and a great red beard.

Dark-eyed, diminutive Nellie was captivated immediately. She thought him the finest looking man she had ever seen and she liked his talk. She asked her brother to introduce her. But Henry, after the fashion of older brothers, could see no reason why General Mussey, a man of prominence well up in his thirties, should be bothered by a chit of a girl like Nellie.

"Besides, General Mussey is a married man with a family," Henry informed his sister. No introduction was forthcoming.

Shortly after this Nellie joined the church and became a teacher in the Sunday school. General Mussey was the superintendent, and they became acquainted. His small daughter was one of the pupils in Nellie's class. But Nellie did not meet General Mussey's wife. She was ill and later that winter she died, leaving General Mussey with two little girls, one a tiny infant.

Delavan Mussey was a son of Reuben Dimond Mussey, who had been professor of medicine at Dartmouth, later at the Ohio Medical College and at Miami Medical College. Young Mussey had sprung from a long line of physicians but he preferred to be a newspaper man. He became a reporter in Cincinnati, Ohio, and, in 1861, went with the Lincoln inaugural party to Washington, D. C. The war soon followed, and Mussey, commissioned a captain, became the mustering officer for the Army of the Cumberland.

Captain Mussey volunteered to raise colored troops in spite of the widespread prejudice against the enlistment of Negroes and the scorn of his fellow officers. But he believed that the Negro as a soldier could prove his ability and thus gain the respect of the nation. And as the war progressed, the need of Negroes became urgent. Mussey mustered in large numbers of them, was made Colonel of the One Hundredth Regiment of colored troops, and later given the rank of Brevet Brigadier-General.

At the close of the war he was ordered to Washington and arrived there the night of Good Friday, April 14. The city was ablaze with lights, streets were gay with color, the people were celebrating the victory, and the President was attending the theater.

Then came the tragedy. Lincoln was shot, and revelry gave way to anxiety. People crowded about the theater, surged against the house where Lincoln lay dying. The city was in turmoil. Troops were called out and all officers ordered to give their services wherever needed.

Mussey was stopping at the Kirkwood House and the Vice-President, Andrew Johnson, was also staying at the Kirkwood, so Mussey devoted himself to the Vice-President's needs. As a result, Mr. Johnson, upon going to the White House as President, took General Mussey along as military secretary.

Excitement in Washington continued at a high pitch. Lincoln's assassin, John Wilkes Booth, was pursued and shot. Conspirators were arrested, tried, and sentenced. Four of them, including a woman, Mrs. Surratt, were condemned to die. Public opinion in general favored this supreme penalty for the three men but there was opposition to the hanging of Mrs. Surratt, partly because she was a woman and partly because of a belief that she was not involved in the actual death plot.

General Mussey was among those favoring clemency for Mrs. Surratt and he hoped the President would stay her execution. But some of the evidence against Mrs. Surratt was strong, and Johnson showed no sign of commuting her sentence. Still, Mussey was hopeful and on the day of the execution he kept his horse and gig waiting at the White House portico so that he might carry the news at once should a reprieve be granted.

That morning Miss Annie Surratt, daughter of the condemned woman, came to plead with the President. But he had given orders that he would see no one, and she asked for General Mussey. The *Evening Star* described the scene. "As soon as the General made his appearance, Miss Surratt threw herself upon her knees before him and, catching him by the coat, with loud sobs and streaming eyes implored him to assist her in obtaining a hearing with the President. General Mussey in as tender a manner as possible informed Miss Surratt that he could not comply with her request as President Johnson's orders were imperative. . . . Upon General Mussey returning to his office Miss Surratt threw herself upon the stair steps where she remained a considerable length of time, sobbing aloud in the greatest anguish. . . ." That afternoon Mrs. Surratt with the three condemned men was hanged.

This case aroused Mussey's interest in legal matters, and some months later he left the White House and the military service and took up the study of law in the office of Mr. A. G. Riddle.

Admission to the bar at the time was comparatively simple. It required in General Mussey's case merely an oral examination by a committee of three, each of whom, quizzing him separately, asked the same questions regarding a case that had recently been given a court decision. Then Mussey began the practice of law.

The fact that he was a lawyer intensified Nellie Spencer's interest in him. Their friendship grew, and June, 1870, found General Mussey a frequent caller at Nellie's home.

That summer, however, when Sara, with true sisterly interest, inquired as to Nellie's suitors and was informed by the observant Sally that a certain red-headed General Mussey, a widower, was becoming very attentive and was in high favor, Nellie was speedy and emphatic in her denials.

"Anyway," she burst out hotly, "his hair is not red. It's golden."

In the fall a much larger number of women students enrolled at the Spencerian Business College, and Nellie's job became more strenuous. Fall, too, brought more and more social events, and she plunged gaily into the whirl. Too gaily. The strain of it began to tell upon her health, and with the coming of the new year she was completely exhausted. She had to give up her work entirely. Her lungs were weak, and her physician advised a change of climate. Nellie had long dreamed of a western trip and now she made plans to go to California as soon as she was a little stronger.

But cupid intervened. General Mussey asked her to marry him. They became engaged, and he gave her an opal ring.

Nellie was very happy, very much in love, and yet . . . The thought of marriage, binding, permanent thing that it was, frightened her. Besides she was not yet twenty-one and there were so many things she had planned to do before settling down to the duties of wifehood and motherhood. And General Mussey was a widower with children. Liberty all at once became very precious. Filled with doubts, Nellie did not announce her engagement and did not wear her ring except when General Mussey was calling.

Delavan Mussey, however, could be as fiery as his hair and he would have no shilly-shallying. "You're not only engaged to me but you're going to marry me," he informed her emphatically.

Thereupon he appeared unexpectedly one Sunday morning and accompanied her to church. That was tantamount to a public announcement of their betrothal, and Nellie at last capitulated. She set the wedding date for June 14, 1871.

The trip west was out of the question now for General Mussey could not leave his law practice. But Nellie's health was a matter of grave concern, and a consultation was held with her physician. He decided that if she were given the proper care she might safely marry and remain in Washington. And General Mussey was well qualified to look after her. He had learned a great deal about medicine and hygiene from his father. He assured Nellie that he would make her well again.

As the wedding date drew near, however, the young woman was in such a wretched physical condition she could scarcely walk. But General Mussey would not consider postponing the wedding ceremony. He was superstitious about that.

June 14 arrived. Nellie at this time was making her home with her brother, Lyman, who through Gen. Garfield, had received an appointment to the State Department. And with her sister-in-law's help, Nellie made ready for her wedding in a dress of sheer white with a long train, trimmings of yards and yards of Valenciennes lace, and a wedding veil with orange blossoms. She carried a bouquet of white flowers, encircled with an edging of stiff white lace paper, very stylish, the gift of Simon Wolf, register of deeds.

General Mussey in a colonial costume, blue swallow-tailed coat with brass buttons, buff vest, and gray trousers, called for her, and together they went to the Church of the New Jerusalem where the ceremony was to be held at high noon, the fashionable hour.

Nellie was so weak and ill that General Mussey, fearing she might faint, had provided himself with a vial of brandy. And she had to be carried up the steps of the church. But with the General's arm supporting her, she managed somehow to walk down the aisle to the altar. The church was crowded with friends and acquaintances. The ceremony began.

Both General Mussey and Nellie objected to the use of the word "obey" in the ceremony and they desired the double ring service, innovations that required considerable changing of the ritual. To further complicate matters, in the absence of the regular pastor, the Rev. Mr. H——— of Baltimore had come down to officiate, and the Rev. Mr. H——— had never before tied the nuptial knot.

He stammered as he groped for the right word. The bride trembled. But General Mussey, knowing full well what he wanted said, deftly assisted the minister, and the service was properly concluded. Ellen Spencer became Ellen Spencer Mussey.

General Mussey's little daughter acted as flower girl, and after the ceremony she insisted upon riding in the carriage with her new mother. They went directly to the Mussey home and law office located on Four-and-One-Half Street, opposite the Court House and Judiciary Square.

Supervising the Mussey household at this time was Miss Lizzie Shellenberger, who had once kept house for Thaddeus Stevens, abolitionist congressman from Pennsylvania, and before that she had been nurse to Miss Olivia Langdon, who married Mark Twain. Miss Lizzie had seen a good deal of life and she was considerably worried about the new wife who was so young and so ill. How would she ever be able to give the children the attention they required?

But Miss Lizzie had been caring for the two little Mussey girls ever since their mother's death and she remained to look after them and the house. And General Mussey kept his young bride on such a strict health program that within a few weeks she was greatly improved. She got on well with the children, too. In fact she revealed so much interest in their welfare from the start that Miss Lizzie's fears disappeared almost at once.

That fall young Mrs. Mussey decided that the vicinity of Four-and-One-Half Street was not satisfactory for the rearing of children and, since General Mussey did not own the house in which they lived, she took some money received from her father's estate and bought a house at Twelfth and

M Streets, where there was a yard and surroundings better suited to the needs of growing children.

To Miss Lizzie this seemed a remarkably fine thing to do. She could hardly find words enough to praise the good sense and business ability of the new wife. It was the beginning of a warm friendship between the two women.

And in the new home, Mrs. Mussey's first child, a son, was born, Oct. 27, 1872. The baby was named Spencer. A husband, home, and children—Mrs. Mussey was filling the prescribed role of woman. And life seemed complete. She had not the slightest thought of anything different.

CHAPTER VI

A NEW WASHINGTON

Washington with its unpaved streets that were either whirling with dust or impassably muddy, its polluted streams, and its general slovenliness, was a source of constant irritation, and arguments for the removal of the national capital grew in intensity. Yet the city made no move to improve conditions. Public works languished and, amidst the uncertainty, business merely marked time. It was an enervating state of affairs.

But at last a few alert citizens organized for action. They schemed to stop the agitation; to develop the District of Columbia according to the vision of its early planners, Washington, Jefferson, and L'Enfant; and to make it all that a Federal city should be.

First of all a change in local government seemed necessary. At this time the District of Columbia had three separate political divisions, Georgetown, the city of Washington, and the county of Washington; and this system had proved wholly inefficient and purposeless. Improvements that had been made were exasperating. Streets were graded but the grades did not match; a few sewers were laid but they ended nowhere; and they were so cheaply constructed that they slumped in at the slightest provocation, sometimes engulfing unwary travelers. Heavy damages resulted, and the sewers had to be rebuilt. But the new construction was as flimsy as the old. Reforms were imperative.

A leader in the movement for an improved capital city was Alexander Robey Shepherd. Starting as a plumber at seventeen, he had risen to prominence as a builder and had become an important figure politically. An aggressive man, possessing stupendous energy and initiative, Shepherd, with his associates, labored for a change in government and, in 1871, Congress passed an act making the District of

Columbia a Territory with a Governor; Board of Public Works; a legislative assembly—Council and House of Delegates; and a Delegate to the House of Representatives.

This triumph found Washington in a festive mood, for the spirit of reform had already brought results. Pennsylvania Avenue had been newly paved with wooden blocks, and Washingtonians were celebrating with a grand carnival that lasted two days.

There were parades on the avenue, races, and scheduled hours for pleasure riding when buggies, closed carriages, open carriages, sulkies, and all manner of vehicles were pressed into service. Everyone wanted to enjoy the luxury of riding on this incredibly smooth new thoroughfare.

At night the avenue was a fairyland with calcium lights, flaming gas jets, colored lanterns hung in trees and on the fronts of houses, gaily illuminated windows, and a gorgeous display of fireworks. Washington was filled with pride. It was growing up.

The first Governor of the District, appointed by President Grant, was Henry D. Cooke, a scholarly man and a member of the banking firm of Jay Cooke and Company. He was from Ohio, as a young man had studied penmanship under Platt Spencer, and when Nellie Spencer became a teacher at the Spencerian Business College, Mr. Cooke brought his daughter there for instruction. Young Mrs. Mussey watched the progress of the territorial government with interest.

But the real chieftain of the new regime was Alexander Shepherd. He was the executive officer of the Board of Public Works, was in charge of improvements, and he began work with a lavish hand. An enormous number of workmen was hired, and streets were torn up in every direction to lay sewers and water mains and to pave with asphaltum and wooden blocks. The District became a labyrinth of excavations and mounting earthworks.

Of prime importance were the street grades. They had to be made uniform, and Washington with its hills and hollows, its ridges and swamps, was a problem. But Mr. Shepherd was dauntless. He simply cut down the hills and filled in the ravines.

As a result certain householders found themselves suddenly pinnacled far above the streets while others were plunged into new-made valleys with once dependable streets rising pertly to scrape acquaintance with second-story windows. Washington began to suffer acute "growing pains." Complaints poured in upon the new government.

The total cost of the proposed improvements had been estimated at a little more than six million dollars, four millions provided for in a bond issue and two millions to be raised by special assessment against the property owners benefited. But Mr. Shepherd's plans were so comprehensive and so drastic that expenses were mounting alarmingly. The territorial government was charged with mismanagement and extravagance and, before it was a year old, it was subjected to a lengthy investigation by Congress.

But little of importance resulted. The Board of Public Works went ahead with its improvements, and the public continued its censure. Some approval was given the Board, however, particularly in the matter of paving streets.

Washington streets were very broad, the cost of paving the entire width was prohibitive, and the Board adopted the plan of paving the central portion and leaving the spaces at the sides to be used by the abutting property owners for planting grass and trees.

A comprehensive plan of tree planting under the supervision of three arborists was an integral part of Shepherd's beautification project, and with these additional parking spaces, Washington's future loveliness seemed assured. And the narrow central paving was quite adequate for the traffic of the seventies.

But this economy did not suffice to save the District purses. Expenditures grew apace, and property owners were burdened with assessments. Still it seemed nothing could stop Mr. Shepherd. Threats of interference by the courts or Congress seemed only to stimulate him to greater action.

One of his projects was the destruction of the old Northern Liberty Market, an unsightly collection of shacks and stands at the intersection of Massachusetts Avenue and K Street. He notified the owners and lessees to move, and provided a new market elsewhere. But the market people objected, and word reached the Board of Public Works that preparations were being made to obtain an injunction against the removal of the Northern Liberty.

A hint was enough for Mr. Shepherd, and he was swifter than a legal process. With cyclonic suddenness he put two hundred laborers to work tearing down the old market and had a force of fifty policemen doing guard duty to prevent interference. Market people were furious, and the story was told that they rushed at once to get a court order to save their property but they were unable to find a District Supreme Court Justice to sign such an order because all the justices in town had been invited to the Shepherd home, Bleak House, just across the District line and were kept well entertained there until the market buildings were destroyed.

In like manner Mr. Shepherd tore up the tracks of the Alexander and Washington Railway Company that had long obstructed the principal approach to the Capitol building. Improvements followed each other in breathless succession. The old myasmic canal was filled in, Tiber Creek was made into a real sewer, miles of sewers were laid, miles of water mains completed, miles and miles of streets paved or graveled, parks developed, hundreds of trees planted. In fact so much was undertaken and so much was accomplished in a short time that expenses, estimated at six millions, had become sixteen millions. The populace was appalled.

About this time Governor Cooke resigned, and Mr. Shepherd himself was appointed Governor. But the territorial regime was doomed. The District was bankrupt; the property owners were faced with ruin; and the government was charged not only with excessive expenditures but with election irregularities. It had become a common practice to import Negroes by the boatload from Maryland and Virginia to swell the vote, and it was said that more than once qualified voters had gone to the polls only to be told that they had already voted.

Congress made a final and drastic investigation, and in June, 1874, the territorial government was abolished and a temporary commission form of government was established with the national government assuming a share in the maintenance of the Capital. With this change Washingtonians lost their right to vote, lost their representative in Congress, and their Legislative Assembly, the Council and the House of Delegates.

The latter in its last session added a final blot to the territorial reputation by indulging in an orgy of plundering government property. Desks, chairs, clocks, mirrors, towels, inkstands, combs, brushes, and soap disappeared. Even an administrative feather duster was appropriated. News of the pillaging leaked out, and a great hubbub ensued. Legislators, however, were quick in their own defense. Desks and chairs, said they, were merely being taken to be repaired and such trifles as brushes and combs had been thrown away because they were worn out.

But it was a bit difficult to account for the feather duster which was seen portruding somewhat rakishly from a certain gentleman's trouser leg. A choice morsel for the nation's wits was this feather duster business and the territorial assembly became known far and wide as the "feather duster" legislature.

It had been a feverish epoch, and Mr. Shepherd as its leader was subjected to bitter accusations. But at final hearings before Congress he was acquitted of all charges against his personal honesty and years later when anger had cooled and Washington had begun to reap the benefits of his improvements—better health, higher property values, increased growth and beauty—Shepherd became a hero. He was accorded honors seldom given people of the District of Columbia, and a statue was put up to memorialize his public work.

Even while Washingtonians had been berating Shepherd, they had begun to feel pride in their improved city and, like a family with a newly decorated house, they wanted to give a party, to strut a bit before their friends and some who possibly were not friends. Opportunity came in the presidential inauguration of March 4, 1873.

The guest list was long and impressive; the governors of all the states were invited—a pretentious innovation. And since, for the first time in history, an inaugural procession could march on a smoothly paved avenue, the decorations must be lavish. Flags, streamers, wreaths, and evergreens were hung in profusion; twenty gaily decked arches spanned the line of march; powerful calcium lights were placed along the avenue to give night a brilliance that would rival the day; and plans were made for a grand inaugural ball. It was to be a glorious coming-out party.

But capricious weather, the bogey of all inaugurations, ushered in March 4 with a polar wave. Events must go on, however. President Grant, in defiance of the weather, rode to the Capitol in an open barouche, to take the oath of office. And paraders, military and civic, resplendent in their uniforms, breasted the arctic winds of the avenue. But not without a price. Marchers dropped in the ranks, victims of extreme temperatures. Men on horseback were almost frozen in their saddles. General Mussey, heading a division of the parade, was so stiff with cold, he had to be taken from his horse. Spectators, too, suffered. First aid was the order of the day and hot whisky was the chief restorative.

Enthusiasm for the inaugural ball somewhat waned. But not with young Mrs. Mussey, for this would be her first big social event since the birth of her child, her first opportunity, too, to attend an inaugural ball with its host of fashionable and important people, and she had been looking forward to it for weeks. With glowing anticipation she planned her toilet. She was going to wear her wedding gown.

The ball, however, was to be given in a new building, a temporary structure of unseasoned lumber, hastily put together for the occasion. It was inadequately heated for such low temperatures, and the supervising architect, A. B. Mullett, who was a friend of General Mussey, warned him to see that his wife dressed warmly. Accordingly General Mussey was adamant. Either Nellie would be sensible or there would be no going to the ball.

Dutifully, regretfully, she put aside the filmy wedding finery, for she could not think of missing the ball. Besides, a ticket had already been bought. It had cost twenty dollars, and Miss Lizzie and Miss Mary Barton, a friend, were going with the Musseys. One ticket was supposed to admit a gentleman and two ladies, but General Mussey, with some adroitness, managed the admission of three ladies.

The ballroom was gay with white muslin, evergreens, flags, and brilliant gas lights; and on the platform where President and Mrs. Grant were receiving were hundreds of canaries to greet the guests with song. But the room was glacial and the poor canaries, too frozen to sing, huddled pitifully in their cages, bills tucked under wings. Guests, blue and shivering, hurried through the formalities of the receiving line and back to dressing rooms to don furs and wraps. Men wore their overcoats, some of them even put on their hats, and the ladies swathed themselves in shawls.

Announcement of supper, served before the dancing began, was received with a burst of enthusiasm because supper would be hot. The repast was a bountiful one with plenty of champagne and claret punch, yet guests for the most part wanted neither of these. They ordered hot drinks, coffee, tea, and chocolate. Even these had to be taken quickly if taken hot for steaming foods were speedily cooled.

Because of the cold the Musseys did not stay for the dancing, and the party was a great disappointment to Mrs. Mussey.

That spring the Musseys moved to Laurel, Maryland. The baby was sickly and the family physician advised the country where a cow could be kept to provide fresh milk. They took a house in Yankee Row, and here Mrs. Mussey watched over her children and enjoyed a pleasant neighborliness with the Laurel housewives. Miss Lizzie milked the cow. She insisted upon doing everything possible to win the new baby to health. And he was soon thriving.

With the expectation of another child, the Musseys returned to the District of Columbia and rented a house in LeDroit Park, a newly opened suburban section that was fenced in, was without streets, and open to none but white residents. Mrs. Mussey's second child, another son, was born December 2, 1874.

She was ill for a long time afterward, and the baby was alarmingly frail. It suffered continually from digestive troubles and made no gain in weight.

Gradually Mrs. Mussey's health returned, but no hope was held out for the baby. At nine months he weighed little more than at birth, and as a last resort the physician suggested trying an old Maryland cure for digestive ailments—ripe peaches.

A queer prescription the parents thought, but they were desperate and the baby was fed peaches. He seemed to improve almost at once. Soon he was eating and growing as a normal child should.

Illnesses and domesticity with all its unending tasks! Yet there was never a time that Mrs. Mussey was not ready to hear whatever her husband had to say of his law cases, and he often talked them over with her. In one case he was associated with General James A. Garfield, and the two men held many conferences at the Mussey home where Mrs. Mussey was an interested listener.

The case was taken to the United States Supreme Court, and Mrs. Mussey went to the hearing, her second visit to this tribunal. She was enraptured at the very thought of listening to a case in charge of her own husband and her friend and when the verdict was given in their favor she was superlatively proud and happy.

But it never occurred to her that she, too, might practice law before this same court; that she, too, might one day win a like success. Such thoughts were beyond her conception. The law was still sacredly masculine.

Yet the admission of a woman to the bar in 1869 had been followed by others, and Washington, too, had its pioneer. In 1873, Mrs. Belva Lockwood was admitted to practice before the Supreme Court of the District of Columbia.

But Mrs. Lockwood was continually being ridiculed. When the tricycle, forerunner of the bicycle, came into vogue, Mrs. Lockwood adopted this means of transportation, the first woman in the District of Columbia to dare to ride a wheel. And newspapers, poking fun at her at every opportunity, caricatured her going about with her bundle of briefs. Many people considered it improper for a woman to ride a wheel, and some of them maintained that if she must ride such a vehicle, she should at least have a shield or screen of some kind to conceal the motion of her limbs. It was most indelicate at the time to speak of a woman as having legs.

Mrs. Lockwood was considered queer. The public thought that any woman who practiced law must be queer. And Ellen Spencer Mussey, in common with the great majority, believed that women who went into this profession were rashly overstepping the bounds of their sex.

Chapter VII

AN EMERGENCY

General Mussey was a fiery Republican and in the Presidential campaign of 1876 he went on the stump to urge the election of Rutherford B. Hayes, whom Mussey had known well in his younger days in Cincinnati, Ohio.

Campaign life was exacting, the weather was hot, and malaria was a common summer epidemic. Mussey had suffered from this malady in the Civil War, and on a tour of West Virginia he again became its victim.

He was forced to return home and was ordered by his physician to take a complete rest. Mrs. Mussey was informed that it would be months before her husband could look after his law practice again.

This was a staggering blow because family finances were always at a low ebb. But the sick husband and four children would have to be provided for, rents would have to be paid, expenses met somehow.

Of major importance, it seemed to young Mrs. Mussey, was her husband's law practice. That would provide some income and it must be kept up so that the General could return to it when he recovered his health.

But who was to look after this law practice? Assuredly, she could not afford to turn it over to another lawyer because she needed every penny available. She even found it necessary to dismiss her husband's clerk.

Only one course, then, seemed open to her. She must go into the law office herself. After all, she did know a great deal about many of the cases, she could attend to the correspondence, confer with clients, and consult General Mussey when necessary. Of course she could not attend to any court cases, but court cases were a small part of the practice. Somehow she would manage, and Miss Lizzie could look after General Mussey and the children.

But nothing save such dire necessity as this could have induced Ellen Spencer Mussey to go into a law office. Indeed, so firmly embedded was her belief that the law was not for women, she was even afraid her own presence in her husband's law office might be detrimental to his profession. And to guard against this, to make it clearly understood that she was not one of those bold women attempting to usurp man's rightful place, she painstakingly explained to everyone that she was merely looking after her husband's law practice until he should be well again.

She hoped people would understand and she was so eager to please, so ready to be helpful, so thoroughly businesslike, that no one seemed to object to her. Clients and lawyers dropped into the Mussey law office quite as often as formerly, some of them perhaps more often, it was so new and diverting to see a woman, especially such a comely, rosy-cheeked young woman, diligently occupying herself with legal principles.

But the law practice that winter of 1876-77 did not thrive. Business in general was somewhat at a standstill, a result of the muddled November elections. Several states had sent in contradictory returns and Republicans had proclaimed the victory for Hayes while the Democrats heralded the success of Tilden. It was a grave situation, and feelings of distrust and unrest pervaded Washington, many people fearing an insurrection and awaiting the outcome to settle matters of importance.

An electoral commission of fifteen members, five from the House of Representatives, five from the Senate, and five from the United States Supreme Court, was appointed to determine the validity of the votes in question, but weeks became months and still no one knew who should be the next President.

During these months of depression Mrs. Mussey had to find ways to reduce expenses, and she moved her family from the suburbs and combined home and law office in a house near Judiciary Square. It was customary for attorneys to have their homes and law offices together, and houses along the west and south sides of the Square were mainly occupied by lawyers who liked the convenience of being near the Court House.

It was necessary, also, for Mrs. Mussey to find other means than the law to provide for her family, and, since the house was large, she took in roomers and boarders. When she heard that a convention of educators was to be held in Washington she went to the Commissioner of Education, General John Eaton, with whom she was acquainted, and asked him to send her delegates in search of rooms. She kept the house filled.

Her days now were a strange mixture of domestic labors and professional duties. Sometimes she left a boy in charge of the office while she attended to household tasks and sometimes she took her work, such as sewing, into the office. Four rapidly growing children and the coming of spring meant the need of many new clothes.

Miss Lizzie did most of the sewing, but it fell to Mrs. Mussey's lot to make the buttonholes, and there were twelve costumes for each child with twenty-nine buttonholes to the costume. Buttonholes and legal matters and legal matters and buttonholes made life a bit dizzying.

At last, two days before inauguration, the electoral commission reached a decision, and Rutherford B. Hayes was announced the victor for the Presidency. Republican leaders, however, were still uneasy. March 4, 1877, fell upon Sunday, and it was the custom under the circumstances to hold the inauguration on the following Monday. But the Republicans were fearful of what might happen in that additional twenty-four hours. Therefore, they took precautionary measures.

In order to prevent any possible coup d'etat by the opposition they had Mr. Hayes sworn in as President on Saturday night, March 3, opinion being against administering the oath on Sunday. And on Monday, for the second time, Mr. Hayes took the oath as part of the regular inaugural ceremonies.

Almost at once business took a more active turn, and Mrs. Mussey plunged into legal activities. Not that she had any desire to make a record for herself. She was merely seeking bread and butter for her family. And General Mussey, though he was much improved, was still unable to take charge of his work.

An important case that came up at this time was a claim against the government concerning a boat that had been appropriated in the Civil War. Such a case had to be settled by Congress, and getting a decision usually meant a long tedious job for the attorney. He must get a Congressman to introduce a bill covering the case and, when it was referred to the proper committee, must keep vigilantly after the members to get a hearing. That required endless tact, patience, and perseverance.

When a hearing was obtained, the bill was reported back favorably or unfavorably; and if favorably, it went on the calendar to be acted upon on a certain date. But even then the case was likely to be ignored unless the attorney kept it fresh in Congressional minds.

Naturally an acquaintance with Congressmen was invaluable, and through her general social life and her family connections Mrs. Mussey knew several Congressmen. Without hesitation she sought their help in this claims case. They seemed willing to assist her and in a surprisingly short time a bill was passed, favoring the Mussey client.

It was Mrs. Mussey's first real legal victory and she was jubilant because the fee was $1500. At last it seemed the proverbial silver lining had appeared. But this feeling of triumph was short-lived. The client, declaring the fee was exorbitant, refused to pay. There was nothing to do but file suit to prevent his collecting his damages, amounting to several thousand dollars, from the government, and Mrs. Mussey put the matter in the hands of an attorney friend.

The client lived out of the city, and Mrs. Mussey, who was not acquainted with him, had given him no inkling that a woman was handling his case, but now he came to Washington, was entertained at the Mussey home, and learned that a woman had successfully put his case through Congress. Quite suddenly, it seemed, all difficulties were smoothed out and the fee was paid in full.

Mrs. Mussey was successful with still other claims cases and, as the months passed, it became increasingly evident that she had a keen aptitude for the law. She found it absorbing, too. But she had no intention whatever of making it a permanent occupation and when, after nearly two years, General Mussey was well enough to take up his practice again, she was quite ready to return to the world's ordained sphere for woman—home and domesticity. That, she thought, was her duty.

But General Mussey was thoroughly shocked when she voiced this decision. Nor would he accept it. "Young woman," he exclaimed, "you've demonstrated your ability in the law and you're going to stay right here."

She was astonished. But it pleased her that he should want her in his office and she needed no further inducement to go on with the law. However, nothing was said about her admission to the bar. General Mussey likely saw no need for that, and Mrs. Mussey, herself, could not yet contemplate anything so radical.

Her duties consisted chiefly of preparing material for briefs, interviewing clients, looking after correspondence, and other routine details. And she completely forgot her fears that her presence would be harmful to the law practice, for clients, lawyers, and business men who frequented the office seemed not the least disturbed because a woman had violated its sacred precincts.

But of course she asked no special consideration because of her sex and did not interfere in any way with their customary masculine comfort. They might sit with their hats on as much as they liked, smoke until the air was blue, chew tobacco, and prop their feet on desks, chairs, or whatever was available, and she brought forth no objections. They felt at home, they discussed their law cases with her, called her "Portia," and treated her as one of them.

She resented the appellation somewhat, for Portia, though she had done a creditable piece of work, was really not a lawyer nor a student of the law. But the name stuck. Mrs. Mussey began now to learn something of the status of her sex. A national bank had failed and the officials, charged with misappropriation of funds, were represented by General Mussey. In helping to prepare the defense, Mrs. Mussey studied the case assiduously from every angle, and the results shocked her. Banks, she discovered, were conducted entirely for men and by men. No women were employed and scarcely any women were depositors.

Bankers, it seemed to Mrs. Mussey, must be extremely lacking in foresight and acumen to overlook half the population when their chief concern was to build up a flourishing business. No wonder they failed. She was sure the officials in this case were not guilty of any criminal intent but simply of poor management. And she undertook a discussion of the banking business with them and other bankers of her acquaintance.

She suggested they hire women clerks, that women clerks would encourage women depositors. She went so far as to advocate the appointment of women on the boards of directors.

But to the bankers such ideas were sheer absurdities. Politely, but none the less forcefully, they informed Mrs. Mussey that women were of no consequence in the business world, that few of them had money, and that certainly no woman was a large enough depositor to justify her appointment as a director.

Besides, maintained the bankers, still politely but even more forcefully, banking was much too profound for the comprehension of the female mind. The business world was not for women. Their place was in the home.

But Mrs. Mussey had begun to question these tenets. For she had gone out of the home, she was doing what had formerly been considered man's work, and she seemed to be doing it with some success, too.

Furthermore, she was positive that neither her home nor her children suffered because of it. To be sure Miss Lizzie was the mainstay of the household, but Mrs. Mussey kept a watchful eye upon its affairs, particularly the welfare of the children. Whatever the demands of the law office, she would not neglect her children. In fact, she believed she was even more devoted to them than she had been. She was proud of her two girls and her two boys. And, like other mothers, she was given to extravagant dreams of the days when they would be young men and young women.

But all of them would not grow up. Early in 1880 the family circle was broken and saddened by the death of little Susan Victoria, a golden-haired whirlwind of energy, aged ten, the younger of the two little girls. At first it was thought that Susie had caught a severe cold, but the physician pronounced it diphtheria.

This disease was not regarded with any great seriousness in the eighties, the house was not put under quarantine, and people were allowed to come and go as usual. When the child died, however, the health officer had the bed and bedding taken away to be destroyed. But the room itself was not fumigated and there was no ban on attendance at the funeral. Queerly enough, too, there seemed to be no spread of the disease.

Scarlet fever and measles were also subjected to very little regulation at this time, but public health laws regarding smallpox were strict. Smallpox patients had to be isolated and a warning flag of yellow flannel or a placard with the word "smallpox" in large letters must be displayed before the house. The health ordinance stated that "It shall be the duty of those in whose dwellings smallpox occurs to fumigate the house and the room of the patient with the fumes of burning sulphur, three times a day; to cleanse and disinfect every part of the dwelling by the free use of chlorinated soda, carbolic acid, bromo chloralum, or such other disinfectant as the Board of Health may direct."

Also, "a cloth the size of a square yard, steeped in a solution of chlorinated soda, carbolic acid, or bromo chloralum," had to be hung in the patient's room and "kept constantly saturated with the said disinfectants."

Ventilation of the sick room was stressed, and the law required that no other person than a nurse who had had the smallpox, or a member of the family, be allowed to enter the patient's room. The patient's clothing, too, must be washed by none except those who had had the smallpox.

Within the next few decades more severe health rulings were made for such diseases as diphtheria, scarlet fever, and measles. When Miss Lizzie died many years after little Susie, Mrs. Mussey wished to bury the two in the same grave because they had been such close comrades in life, but permission to open the child's grave was refused because the death record specified a contagious disease.

The years were passing and still no step was taken toward Ellen Spencer Mussey's admission to the bar. But a few more women were practicing law and in 1879, Mrs. Belva Lockwood had been admitted to practice before the Supreme Court of the United States.

Women were making progress, and now Mrs. Mussey herself began to wish that she might be a full-fledged lawyer. But she felt that she had an insuperable handicap. She was timid, so timid that the very thought of speaking in public filled her with terror. Often General Mussey had urged her to talk at church meetings and other small gatherings, but she could not do that. Then of course she could never go to court, never argue in a client's behalf, never assume the full responsibility of a lawyer.

Still the desire to be a lawyer kept creeping back again and again. But she did not speak of this to her husband.

Chapter VIII

SOCIAL LIFE

The new President, Rutherford B. Hayes, and General Mussey had become friends when they were members of the Literary Club of Cincinnati, an organization famous for its eminent members and for having furnished a large number of officers to the Union Army during the Civil War. And shortly after Mr. and Mrs. Hayes moved to the White House, the Musseys went to call.

They were received quite as informally as at other homes, and Mrs. Hayes, like others who have acquired a fine new home, took her guests on an inspection tour, showed them especially the rooms on the second floor. She was delighted with the White House and spoke warmly of the orderliness and cleanliness in which she found it.

Not all newcomers could say as much, for some of them in the past had considered it necessary to give the Executive mansion a thorough cleaning before they could accept it as a home. But Mrs. Grant was a meticulous housekeeper and she had everything in perfect order for her successor, even had the lace curtains washed and mended. She would have preferred buying new ones, which were badly needed, but no funds were available for that purpose. Mrs. Grant, too, planned meals for the new arrivals, not only luncheon for inauguration day, which was customary, but dinner for that evening and breakfast the next morning.

A most happy reception, Mrs. Hayes observed, after all the pre-inaugural perplexities when she and Mr. Hayes had not known whether they would go to the White House or stay in Ohio. This eleventh-hour selection as White House hostess had given Mrs. Hayes no time to prepare for her new duties or even to get ready a suitable wardrobe, she told Mrs. Mussey. But Mrs. Hayes was looking very well in a black silk dress on this particular evening and Mrs. Mussey complimented her on it.

Mrs. Hayes laughed. The dress was an old one, she said, that had been hurriedly remade, turned upside down, inside out, and hindside before, just like the minister's wife's proverbial best gown.

A visit to the White House could be quite as pleasantly gossipy as a visit to any other home, Mrs. Mussey discovered. She and General Mussey went often to see Mr. and Mrs. Hayes and were usually entertained in the red parlor or the library. Sometimes the Musseys attended small parties at the White House, and at one of these, General William Tecumseh Sherman was a guest.

Mrs. Mussey and other young women gathered about General Sherman as he told of early soldiering experiences in Florida. Army life with its long marches in cold drizzling rains and its monotonous rations of hard-tack, salt pork, and black coffee, had dampened the spirits of the young men, and General Sherman said they fell to talking one evening of the good things they would like to eat. The company cook, overhearing them, promised as a special treat the next morning for breakfast, nothing less than hot chicken pie. The men scoffed loudly. Well they knew the impossibility of such a delicacy.

But aroused the next morning at three o'clock for an early march, they were greeted by the amazing and unmistakable odor of chicken and there was the chicken pie as promised. It was delicious, the General said, and not until long afterward did the men learn that their "chicken pie" had been made from hard-tack, salt pork, and alligator meat which had been cooked together all night in an improvised oven.

Shortly after becoming President, Mr. Hayes gave a dinner in honor of friends of the Literary Club of Cincinnati, and this dinner became a sensation. No liquor was served. Conventional Washington was shocked. And certain officials in dismay at the idea of a liquorless White House, predicted divers calamities, loss of national prestige, and even rifts in international relations should such a policy be continued.

Storms of protest and ridicule descended upon Mr. and Mrs. Hayes, but they had not served liquor in their home in Ohio and they saw no reason for changing their habits simply because they had moved into the White House. Mrs. Hayes was held mainly responsible for this temperance stand and in some circles she was derisively called "Lemonade Lucy."

There came a dinner at the White House, however, at which some of the guests were sure the total abstinence rule had been broken for the orange dessert seemed strangely exhilarating. Rum must have been used in its making. But upon inquiry it was found that the dessert contained no spirituous liquors, that it was merely the concoction of a clever cook.

Nevertheless liquor was served at one dinner given during the Hayes administration. When the Grand Dukes Alexis and Constantine of Russia visited Washington and were entertained at the White House, the question of liquor was left to the State Department, and since this was purely an official event, the Secretary of State, William E. Evarts, decided that wine should be served.

The next administration brought General and Mrs. James A. Garfield to the White House. But the times were unhappy politically. Garfield had been the dark horse at the Republican convention in 1880, had won the nomination chiefly through the last-minute support of the strong Grant forces, headed by Roscoe Conkling, Senator of New York, and under the circumstances it was expected that Mr. Garfield would make some returns in the matter of appointments. Besides, it was customary to consult a Senator's wishes in the matter of appointments within his state. But Mr. Garfield in filling the important office of Collector of the Port of New York not only ignored Mr. Conkling's preference but appointed a man whom Conkling opposed.

A bitter controversy resulted with the Republican party dividing into two hostile camps. Senator Conkling resigned from office, also New York's junior Senator, Thomas R.

Platt, often called "Me-too" Platt because he echoed so many of Conkling's dictums. And Washington excitedly joined in the fray.

President Garfield was worried over the situation. At a White House reception to which the Musseys were invited shortly after inauguration, Mrs. Mussey noted the President's anxiety at once. When James G. Blaine, the new Secretary of State, arrived, President Garfield asked with much concern, "Any news from the seat of war?" referring to the trouble with Conkling. It disturbed Mrs. Mussey to see her girlhood hero in such difficulties. She wished he had paid more attention to the political amenities.

Several government officials were in attendance at this reception, and Mrs. Mussey made the acquaintance of Robert Todd Lincoln, Secretary of War, and Morris Waite, Chief Justice of the United States Supreme Court. Mr. Waite had heard of this young woman who had gone into her husband's law office, and he asked to be introduced to her. She felt highly honored. It was becoming more and more delightful to go to the White House.

But the Garfield's sojourn there was brief. Though political affairs, as the weeks passed, grew somewhat calmer, enmities still existed, and Charles Guiteau, insane office seeker who had become a daily nuisance at the White House (it was the day when office seekers thronged to the Executive mansion), became obsessed with the idea that he must reunite the Republican factions and save the nation. According to his warped conclusions the only way to do this was to get rid of the President. Guiteau shot Garfield the morning of July 2 as the President was walking through the Baltimore and Potomac depot to board a train for his alma mater at Williamstown, Mass.

The Musseys, who lived near the station, heard the crowds running through the streets shouting, "The President has been shot." And flashing instantly across Mrs. Mussey's mind came the memory of Garfield expressing the wish that he might die as Lincoln had died. Garfield was still living, however, there was hope that he might recover, and he lingered on through a dreary summer. But the end came Sept. 19, 1881.

Chester A. Arthur, polished society and club man of New York City, became the new President. He was a new type in the White House and it underwent marked changes. Not until wagonload after wagonload of old furnishings had been hauled away from the Executive mansion and the place thoroughly renovated and redecorated with gay pomegranate hangings, new upholstered furniture, potted palms, and other furnishings requisite to New York society homes, did President Arthur take up his residence there. He even had a smoking room added.

Washingtonians were agog at all this elegance, and they thronged to the public receptions to see this splendor with their own eyes and to compare the new occupants with former ones. It was a choice pastime of capital city residents.

Following the Civil War, military societies were numerous, and General Mussey belonged to the Grand Army of the Republic, the Society of the Army of the Cumberland, and the Military Order of the Loyal Legion. Reunions and celebrations were rife. One of the popular summer diversions was to go by boat down the Potomac River to Marshall Hall, former home of the Marshall family, which had been turned into a riverside resort and was famous for its lovely grounds and good food, particularly its planked shad. It was well known for its liquor, too, for beer and wines were considered indispensable to the success of most such outings and all pleasure resorts featured their liquors.

Mrs. Mussey thoroughly enjoyed military society celebrations because they meant opportunity to associate with the heroes of the war. At one Marshall Hall shad bake she sat at the right of General Phil Sheridan and he carved the shad, serving her with what he declared were the very choicest bits. Which of course made the occasion one to be remembered.

When military societies went visiting they were always heartily welcomed, and at a convention which the Musseys attended in Rochester, N. Y., the whole city kept open house, showing the guests through industrial establishments, the parks, art galleries, cemeteries, beer gardens, breweries, and even the brewery stables that housed the massive horses used to haul Rochester's beer.

This city was the home of Susan B. Anthony, and she called upon Mrs. Mussey at her hotel. The two women had met several times since their first acquaintance at the suffrage meeting in 1870 when Nellie in such terror had sat upon the platform, and though the latter had not become active in the suffrage cause, as a young woman who had dared to go into her husband's law office she had won Miss Anthony's interest.

True feminist that she was, Miss Anthony never lost an opportunity to encourage women in their new ventures nor did she ever let pass unchallenged any slight upon the competence of her sex. One of Mrs. Mussey's friends at this meeting inadvertently became the victim of an arrow from the Anthony quiver.

Three army men, Doctor B———, Lieutenant K———, and Major W———, had accompanied the Musseys to Rochester. They were with Mrs. Mussey when Miss Anthony arrived and they remained to enjoy the noted suffragist's pithy conversation. When she left, Lieutenant K——— went with her. They were occupied with a discussion and it was not until they had gone some distance that it suddenly occurred to Miss Anthony that Lieutenant K——— must be intending to escort her home. She stopped and asked him pointblank if that was his intention.

He admitted that it was.

"Why, I know my way home quite well," exclaimed Miss Anthony, "I've found it by myself hundreds and hundreds of times and I'm quite able to do it again."

The Lieutenant could do nothing but return to his hotel.

After leaving Rochester, General and Mrs. Mussey visited Albany and went for a sightseeing trip to the Capitol. Their guide asked General Mussey if he would like to shake hands with the Governor, Grover Cleveland, who was the

Mrs. Mussey at the Age of 38.

Democratic candidate for the Presidency, and General Mussey assented eagerly. But Mrs. Mussey, possibly because she was a woman and had no vote, was not included in the invitation and she had to content herself with an exhaustive inspection of the President-to-be from the doorway of his office. When General Mussey returned she asked why he had not suggested that she, too, go in to meet Mr. Cleveland.

"Why, I didn't suppose you would shake hands with a man like Cleveland," cried General Mussey. Unfavorable stories of the Democratic nominee were in circulation and many people had the idea that he was a boor, but General Mussey declared he found Mr. Cleveland very pleasant and courteous.

When Cleveland was elected, the Democrats prepared for a mighty inauguration. It had been twenty-eight years since a Democrat had been made President, and organizations and individuals vied for honors. Some of the Congressmen even quarreled. Mrs. Mussey on a visit to the House to learn the fate of a certain bill was greeted by a heated discussion of the inaugural ceremonies. Certain of the gentlemen declared the Senators were being favored, and one Congressman from West Virginia contended vehemently that he was not going to be a little dog under the wagon.

A woman sitting next to Mrs. Mussey in the gallery was greatly disturbed that Congressmen should be occupied with such a controversy and she remarked caustically, "I hope Georgia will comport itself with dignity."

The inauguration was a triumph. Hosts of Democrats were in the Capital. Tammany braves in full glory paraded the streets, and for the first time since the Civil War, gray-clad troopers of the South marched on the avenue. General Fitzhugh Lee was an imposing figure on his ebon charger at the head of the Virginia columns. Even nature was in accord with the occasion, and the day was one of perfect spring weather.

Cleveland was a bachelor and his sister, Miss Rose Cleveland, became the White House hostess. Miss Cleveland was interested in intellectual pursuits and not much concerned about the dictates of fashion, and at first her clothes and her coiffure somewhat disturbed some of the visitors. But she was so charming and warm-hearted that in no time at all she had completely won the hearts of Washingtonians. She held many afternoon receptions, and Mrs. Mussey went as often as her work at the law office would permit.

When the announcement was made that Mr. Cleveland was to marry Miss Frances Folsom, of Buffalo, N. Y., and that Miss Cleveland would leave the White House, Washington was filled with regret, and her last reception brought a huge and unexpected crowd. Everybody, it seemed, wanted to take advantage of this last opportunity to see Miss Cleveland.

No arrangements had been made to care for so many people, and the rooms were so crowded and uncomfortable that guests prepared to leave as soon as they had greeted their hostess. But exits were blocked by crowds that were still coming. Not a door was accessible. But several Civil War Generals were present, among them General Philip Sheridan, and Generals, naturally, had had experience in getting out of tight places. They bethought themselves of a window, drafted stools and chairs into service, and gallantly assisted the ladies in a somewhat undignified but gleeful departure from the White House.

Sunday night suppers were popular in Washington, and the Musseys were guests occasionally of Mrs. E. D. E. N. Southworth, well known novelist of the time, who belonged to the same church the Musseys did and often invited the members and their friends to her home overlooking the Potomac and the Georgetown harbor. Mrs. Mussey thought that Mrs. Southworth was a bit queer, but her suppers were always bountiful and she gave interesting impersonations from her writings.

Sometimes the Musseys received church members at their home near Judiciary Square. Entertainment at these parties varied, but at one of them held in the early eighties, the sole diversion of the evening was supplied by a new and sensational instrument. It was a telephone which the Musseys had just had installed.

Washington had its first telephone in October, 1877. It was a line connecting the office of the chief signal officer of the army with Fort Whipple, later known as Fort Myer, across the Potomac in Virginia. A little later the White House and some of the government offices were equipped with telephones, but in general capital city residents were skeptical about this fantastic means of communication and promoters had a difficult time convincing people that the telephone was practical and needed no skill in its operation.

Telephones were so rare at the time of the Mussey party that most of the guests had never used one. Eagerly they took turns at the transmitter. And since so few people had telephones, the telephone operator had to be the butt of most of these experiments. The same thing was happening wherever a telephone was being installed, the beginning possibly of that bitter and eternal discord that was to mark so many of the relations between central and the general public. But the Musseys' "telephone" party was a great success.

With the advent of summer, social events became fewer in number. Though Washington, following the regime of Alexander Shepherd, was so much more healthful than it had been, the heat was intense, and all who possibly could left the city. But the Musseys, like many others, had to stay in town because of their work. There were compensations, however.

Cooling boat rides could be taken down the river to Marshall Hall and up the river by canal or river road was Cabin John, a tavern with breezy verandas, cupolas, and observation towers, affording diverting views of the surrounding country. Washingtonians went to Cabin John for picnics, fishing parties, Sunday morning breakfasts, and chicken dinners. The tavern was famous for its liquors and it boasted a head waiter who spoke seven languages.

Many summer resorts were near, too, on the Chesapeake Bay and its lovely tributary streams, and in the mountains to the northwest. In the Blue Ridge was Harpers Ferry, picturesquely enthroned at the confluence of two mighty rivers, the Potomac and the Shenandoah, and overlooking the meeting grounds of three states, Maryland, Virginia, and West Virginia. Excursions to Harpers Ferry were popular. General Mussey liked to go there to fish.

And within the District of Columbia, itself, were numerous refreshing oases, the beer gardens. Usually located beside a saloon or a brewery with little tables under the trees or open sky, these gardens were the gathering places of the populace on hot afternoons and evenings.

On E Street was Abner's, where the Musseys and other professional and business people liked to go for evening dinner. Near Dupont Circle was Heurich's, under the management of a brewer who made a point of using the best malts from Ohio, Wisconsin, and Canada in the manufacture of his beer and invited chemical tests of its purity. Near the outskirts of the city on Seventh Street was Scheutzens, a favorite family outing place on Sunday afternoons. Beer gardens were a colorful part of the times. It was the heyday of the eighties.

Chapter IX

THE GOAL

Toward the latter part of the eighties, the Musseys took a more desirable residence on K Street. They continued to move in pleasant social circles, their children were growing up and being educated, and life flowed along smoothly and agreeably. Thus it offered little or no fillip to attainment, and Mrs. Mussey made no effort to become a member of the bar. Besides, women of the law were still the butt of public scorn and ridicule.

But General Mussey was nearing sixty, he often complained of not feeling well, and he began to depend more and more upon Mrs. Mussey to attend to things at the office. She herself was not robust. She had not been in good health since the birth of her last baby, and her physician had advised an operation, but General Mussey feared she could not withstand the effects of an anesthetic and nothing was done. Since she was keeping up with her daily work and General Mussey, too, was usually at the office, neither of them saw any cause for alarm nor any reason to fear that life would not continue in the same comfortable routine.

But in the spring, the eldest son, Spencer, a young man of eighteen, home from Lehigh University for a vacation, was taken suddenly ill. Washington was unseasonably warm, and Spencer took cold. Pneumonia developed and death came quickly. It was a heartbreaking loss to both parents and General Mussey through shock and grief began to fail noticeably.

Within the next few months tragedy visited the family with breath-taking rapidity. Mrs. Mussey's brother, Henry, died, a victim of malaria. And General Mussey, forced at last to give up all semblance of law practice, became seriously ill. Soon, he, too, was taken from her.

These were dark, soul-rending days, and to Ellen Spencer Mussey it seemed the end of things for her. But a family friend of long standing, General John Eaton, who had been with General Mussey in his illness, crystalized Mrs. Mussey's duty unforgetably. "You must be the woman your husband believed you to be," he told her.

Often General Mussey had declared that she was equal to anything. Now came the supreme test. In spite of sorrow, ill health, and obstacles, she must somehow provide for herself and her family. She must go on. Steadfastly she clung to this thought.

Yet at the age of forty-two, after sixteen years in a law office, she was still not a lawyer. The full realization of this handicap had come to General Mussey a few days before his death and he had expressed the wish that he might even yet have strength "to go down and do justice to my wife"—arrange for her admission to the bar. But it had been too late.

No better course seemed open to her, however, than to go on with the law for she felt by this time that she belonged to it. She decided to become a member of the bar.

At once she was plunged into the current of prejudice and opposition to women of the law. She was accused of trying to be spectacular, of seeking the limelight, and she was warned that she could never make a success of the law.

One friend, a man who believed that marriage or a succession of marriages was woman's sole duty and that a woman's chief concern must be to garner her matrimonial assets, was shocked at Mrs. Mussey's decision. "Surely," he cried, "you're not going on with the law! No man wants to marry a woman lawyer."

"Well, I don't want to marry any man," declared Ellen Spencer Mussey. Not that she disliked men. In fact she was very fond of their society. But there were other things beside marriage to be considered now.

Another friend who held a responsible position with the government offered Mrs. Mussey a place as government clerk.

"What will the salary be?" she asked.

"Not more than nine hundred dollars a year, to start with."

"I can't send a boy to college on that," announced Mrs. Mussey with finality.

"But you can't make a success of the law," contended her friend. "No woman can."

Time had been when she would have believed him, but sixteen years in a law office had made her less credulous, less subjected to the ancient dictums. And her goal was burning brightly ahead of her now.

Besides, friends at the bar were encouraging. Men who knew her and her work said, "We shall treat you as one of us." Ross Perry, A. S. Worthington, Walter Davidge, J. J. Darlington, Harry Davis, and others offered to stand by her.

And in his will, General Mussey had appointed two special advisers, Job Barnard, who later became associate justice of the District Supreme Court, and Nathaniel Wilson. They saw no reason why she should not go on with the law and they simply recommended that she take a law partner, to look after court cases and other work with which she was unfamiliar, until she should become a member of the bar. Accordingly, she formed a partnership with Mr. Jacob Lichliter.

By this time her health was wretched, but in spite of her physician's advice that she have an operation, she set herself the task of becoming a member of the bar. And that was no longer the simple process of an oral examination. Formal written examinations were required, and it seemed to Mrs. Mussey the best preparation for this rigid test was a course at a law school. In the fall of 1892 she applied for admission to the law school of the National University in Washington.

But the National University was not accepting women in its law classes and it refused Mrs. Mussey. Under an early charter women had been admitted, and Mrs. Belva Lockwood, Washington's first woman of the law, had been graduated from this school, but a later ruling barred women. The officials declared that men objected to women in their law classes and that women therefore had a deterring effect upon the enrollment.

Considerably dismayed but still hopeful, Mrs. Mussey sought admission to the law school of Columbian College, later known as George Washington University. Here, too, women were denied entrance, but Mrs. Mussey's request was referred to the Board of Trustees.

The verdict came back promptly. Columbian College would accept no women in its law classes. Women had not the mentality to study law, said the august members of the Board.

Certain men of the school who knew Mrs. Mussey and her work sent a petition to the Board asking for a reversal of its decision, but the petition was rejected.

Such were the hindrances to a woman's knowledge of the law. And through worry and disappointment, Mrs. Mussey's physical condition grew steadily worse. Her suffering became so acute it was difficult to go on with her work, and finally her physician warned her of dangerous complications unless she had an operation at once. She could do nothing but submit.

It meant three weary months in bed and even then her health was slow to return, for she had prodded herself to the very limits of physical endurance. And the anxiety over her position in the law did not help matters.

But there was the pressing need of work to be done, of looking after herself and her family and there was Miss Lizzie, the faithful standby, giving encouragement and the best of nursing care. Gradually Mrs. Mussey improved.

And once more she must tackle the problem of gaining admission to the bar. Weak as she still was from her illness, the ordeal of a written examination in the law loomed as a veritable nightmare. How was she ever to prepare for it? Regretfully she thought of the past, of the day more than twenty-five years before when the South Bend attorney had asked her to study law in his office and to become a member of the bar. If she had accepted that opportunity, or if in all the sixteen years she had actually been in a law office . . . But self-reproach was of no help now. What was she to do?

Then quite suddenly and startlingly, fortune smiled upon Mrs. Mussey. Her sister-in-law, Sally Spencer, brought Mrs. Mussey's plight to the attention of Judge MacArthur, formerly associate justice of the District Supreme Court, and he took the matter up with the court.

The Justices were much concerned. They had been under the impression that Mrs. Mussey was already a member of the bar. They made an investigation and, because of her long experience in the profession, decided that an informal oral examination would be sufficient to test her knowledge of the law. An examining committee of three, Job Barnard, Walter Davidge, and S. S. Henkle, was appointed, and Mr. Davidge acted for the committee.

Mrs. Mussey was still not well enough to go out, so Mr. Davidge obligingly came to her home, questioned her about the common law, general reading, and the subject of specific performance. She passed the examination with ease, and Mr. Davidge recommended her admission to the bar. Soon word came that she was to appear in court to take the oath.

That was a momentous day. Even her black and tan dog, Jack, seemed to sense the import of it. Though he usually did not accompany her, on this occasion he leaped and barked frantically, coaxing to share this adventure. She tried to dissuade him for after all a court of law was hardly the place for a dog. But Jack would not be denied, and when the cab arrived that was to take her to court, he dashed into it and settled himself proudly on the seat beside her. At the Court House, however, he was content to remain outside and wait for her.

The oath was quickly administered, and Ellen Spencer Mussey on March 28, 1893, six weeks before her forty-third birthday, was at last a member of the bar.

But she had not yet conquered her timidity.

Chapter X

GROWTH

E. S. Mussey, successor to R. D. Mussey—this was the name Ellen Spencer Mussey chose to begin her career as a full-fledged lawyer. Because of the general skepticism regarding women who had broken into occupations once held exclusively by men, she had learned that it was advisable to use her initials to disguise somewhat the fact that she was a woman, particularly in handling cases from outlying regions.

But so far as the actual practice of law was concerned she continued as before, making no effort to assume full responsibility. Court cases and other legal matters to which she was unaccustomed she left entirely to her partner.

In the fall of 1893 he dissolved the partnership. At once Mrs. Mussey hurried to her advisers to get help in forming a new partnership.

But they said, "You don't need a partner. Depend upon yourself."

It seemed amazing advice. Yet it gave her a strange new confidence in herself. She decided to act upon it.

As she made ready for her first appearance in court, however, she was filled with terror, though it was merely probate court and very informal. Presiding over it were associate justices of the District Supreme Court, Judge C———, who according to court house wits was always sorry he could not decide in favor of the attorneys on both sides, and Judge H———, who was said to be sorry he had to give an opinion in favor of either side.

Often Mrs. Mussey had laughed at these comments but now that she must actually face one of the judges in court, her knees shook frightfully. She could hardly walk.

Just what happened at that session of court she could never recall afterward but somehow she got through the ordeal and knew instinctively that she had done well. And she realized, too, that, after all, it had been a very simple and easy procedure.

Mrs. Mussey hired a man clerk. It was difficult to find a woman law clerk of experience, and besides, it was the day when numerous men seemed unable to forget sex and take women seriously in their new activities in the professional and business world and in dealing with such brethren Mrs. Mussey felt that the presence of a man clerk was a safeguard.

Her problem was to build up a clientele. Though the majority of General Mussey's clients remained with her, some of them did withdraw their business because they objected to a woman. Sex, she found, played a vital part in the practice of law. While some people were utterly opposed to a woman of the bar, others sought her services simply because she was a woman. They thought she would charge smaller fees than a man. It was so customary to get women to work for less money than men. But Mrs. Mussey made it plain that fees were not a matter of sex, that they must be based entirely upon the nature of the work and the ability of the client to pay.

Seeking her services, too, for no other reason except that she was a woman, were men who had become involved in difficulties with women. These men thought that if a woman accepted such a case it would add weight to their defense and have a favorable influence upon the court. But Mrs. Mussey refused their cases.

To enlarge her practice she took a great variety of business such as rentals and collections. The latter was not easy and one case that she had was particularly difficult but the fee offered was liberal and under the name E. S. Mussey, she wrote a sharp letter, peremptorily demanding payment. Her clerk warned her that this would get her into trouble, that the debtor in question was a tough customer. But she sent the letter.

Shortly afterward, a rotund little man came into her office, furiously brandished her letter, and clamored angrily for "this E. S. Mussey." With all the calmness she could assume, she made herself known.

Dumfounded, the man stared at her. Then all at once he began to laugh and presently he was paying the bill though he admitted with a few vigorous exclamations that he had had no such intention when he came. And before he left, he engaged Mrs. Mussey to take a case for him.

Her practice grew. But she refused absolutely to take divorce cases. They were unpleasant, meant notoriety, and brought little pay. One day an attorney friend, W. J. Newton, sent a divorce case to her. She declined it as she had all others.

Mr. Newton took her to task about this. "Young woman," he expostulated, "you've got to take divorce cases. All beginners should."

She was sensitive to reproof and very eager for approbation. Besides Mr. Newton was a respected member of the bar. Perhaps he was right. She accepted the next divorce case offered her, that of a woman acquaintance. But it involved many odious details and Mrs. Mussey became apprehensive. She asked Mr. Newton's help and he agreed to assist her. He was away on a vacation, however, when the case came up for a hearing.

Thoroughly distressed and certain that she could not go through this ordeal alone, Mrs. Mussey went to the Judge, Charles C. Cole, who was to preside that morning, and asked him to have the case postponed until Mr. Newton's return. Judge Cole was her friend and she felt sure he would grant this request.

But instead, Judge Cole rebuked her sternly. "Stand on your own feet," he commanded.

Under the sting of that she had to go ahead with the case. She presented her arguments and she won a favorable decision.

Afterward she was grateful to Judge Cole, painful though his lesson had been, for another bogey had been slain. Never again did she refuse divorce cases because of repulsive details and never again did she fear a court appearance.

In 1893 Mrs. Mussey was appointed a delegate by her church to attend a parliament of religions held in Chicago in connection with the Columbian Exposition and she had to read a paper on the work of women in the church. This was her first public appearance, and the thought of it made her almost ill with fear. But she forced herself to go through with it. Afterward she felt a little more courageous.

The visit to Chicago was full of significance. The women's movement was gaining in momentum. The International Council of Women had recently been formed; also the National Council which had held its first triennial convention in 1891 with forty organizations of women represented; the General Federation of Women's Clubs was being organized; and for this World's Fair, Congress, through the skillful maneuvering of Susan B. Anthony and Elizabeth Cady Stanton, had actually authorized the appointment of a "Board of Lady Managers."

Headed by Mrs. Bertha Honore Palmer, this Board planned a great World's Congress of representative women which was held in connection with the Fair and which brought together the women of twenty-seven countries and 126 organizations. Thousands upon thousands of women, and men, too, attended the meetings. Women's activities and women's accomplishments were to the fore.

Even woman suffrage, so frowned upon that it had been given but one session, was arousing so much interest that extra meetings had to be held, and its valiant leader, Miss Anthony, once so ridiculed and defamed, became the veritable luminary of the Women's Congress. When she talked crowds stormed the meetings, and when she appeared at other meetings, the crowd broke into the discourse of the speaker on the platform to do Miss Anthony honors.

Many women were being acclaimed. Never before had Mrs. Mussey seen such gatherings of gifted women and never had she heard of women receiving such plaudits. Her own former teacher and associate, Charlotte Emerson, now Mrs. Brown, was taking a prominent part in the General Federation of Women's Clubs. Mrs. Mussey felt inspired.

And she saw clearly that organization was the secret of this advancement of women, that organization was the open sesame to power.

Up to this time she had not been a club woman, had had very little interest in societies other than those to which her husband had belonged, but she returned to Washington resolved to become active in women's organizations. She was fully aware of the importance of this professionally, for above all else, club work offered an opportunity to become known and if she was ever to be a success in the law, she must become known.

Women's clubs thrived in Washington but most of them were devoted to social, cultural, and charitable pursuits. Organizations of business and professional women such as came into being in later years were unknown. In fact in some circles it was considered not quite nice for a woman to earn her own living and one exclusive club refused membership to women who went forth to business.

At one of its meetings this society engaged a Congressman friend of Mrs. Mussey to give a talk, and he asked her to come to hear him. But that was impossible because she was a working woman. Other organizations, however, were not so prejudiced, and Mrs. Mussey joined the Legion of Loyal Women, a patriotic society, and a little later she became a member of the Daughters of the American Revolution.

She devoted herself especially to the work of the Legion, soon she was made its president, and the work of this office developed her ability as nothing else had done. But she was still woefully timid, and in 1895 when she was assigned as delegate and speaker at the second convention of the National Council of Women, to be held in Washington, she was filled with dismay.

A notable gathering, this National Council was, with representatives from all parts of the country, white women and black women, Jewish women and Gentile, suffragist and anti-suffragist, some of the most brilliant and cultured women of the land. "How was she ever to face this galaxy of talent?" Mrs. Mussey asked herself.

Her speech, "What the Flag Has Cost Woman," was scheduled for the afternoon of Washington's Birthday, Feb. 22, and Mrs. Mussey, with a feeling of total inadequacy, took her place with the other speakers on the platform. Out in front was that vast and terrifying sea of faces. She felt ill. And her talk was toward the end of the program. It seemed the agony of that long afternoon would never end.

At last, she heard her own name called. She was appalled, and her legs shook so that it seemed they would give way under her as she stood up and walked to the speaker's place. But the audience was waiting. She had to begin. Had to make herself heard, too. Back somewhere in the last row of the gallery sat her daughter, delegated to report how well she could hear the speech. Mrs. Mussey concentrated on that back seat.

And on the stage behind her sat Susan B. Anthony, who had just celebrated her seventy-fifth birthday. Seasoned campaigner that she was, Miss Anthony knew how to help the terrified beginner and always at just the right moment, Miss Anthony whispered reassuringly, "You're doing all right. They can hear you."

When Mrs. Mussey's voice grew husky, Miss Anthony turned to those beside her and said, "Girls, get the child a drink of water." Mrs. Mussey began to feel more comfortable and presently the audience was giving her that greatest stimulus of all—applause.

She talked patriotism. Though the Civil War was long past, there were still folks who waved the Confederate flag and she urged that they put it away with such treasures as the little shoes baby used to wear. The crowd approved heartily, and at the close of her speech she was given a warm ovation.

When she left the platform, Miss Anthony followed, took Mrs. Mussey in her arms and said, "My child, you've done fine."

Achievement—that was a conqueror of timidity and never again was Mrs. Mussey afraid to speak in public. At the convention of the General Federation of Women's Clubs in Philadelphia she led in a discussion from the platform. But when she was asked to give a political speech in the Presidential campaign of 1896, she was decidedly reluctant.

That summer she attended the law school of Cornell University. Cornell did not object to women as law students, and though she was the only woman in a class of seventy-five, no one seemed to be disturbed about it. When the course ended and the students were being asked to speak at various neighborhood events as was the custom, she was invited to Newfield to give a talk on McKinley's candidacy.

She was not a political speaker and she hardly felt equal to that, but when she was informed that no one would be at the meeting except the members of the Brown family, she accepted.

The Brown family, however, proved to be five hundred strong. But she gave her speech. She had known McKinley as a Congressman from Ohio, she was a staunch Republican, and she was eager for his election.

Because she was a woman of the law, she was the object of much curiosity and comment at this meeting and she overheard one man say, "Why she's real good looking even if she is a lawyer." Another observed, "She don't talk like the squire down to the village." For which Mrs. Mussey was thankful when she met the squire.

Small towns and country districts invariably regarded women of the law as peculiar or abnormal creatures, and Mrs. Mussey encountered this attitude frequently. She had many cases in outlying regions, some of them through her work with the Legations of Norway and Sweden for whom she acted as counsel, a practice she had retained following General Mussey's death.

One of these cases involved property near Lynchburg, Virginia. Mrs. Mussey carried on all preliminary work by correspondence with the administrator of the estate but when it came time for a final settlement in court, it was necessary for her to go to Lynchburg. The state of Virginia did not admit women to the bar, and aware of the general attitude in such regions, Mrs. Mussey felt it unwise to give out advance information that she was a woman. She knew that as E. S. Mussey she could be admitted by comity to act for this estate and she made her arrangements accordingly. The judge of the court, therefore, had no inkling that Attorney Mussey was a woman.

Naturally her arrival was a shock. But the judge merely looked his astonishment. He said nothing, and Mrs. Mussey presented her case. It was quickly settled, and then the judge came down from his bench, shook hands with Mrs. Mussey, and told her that he would gladly make arrangements for her at any time she had occasion to bring a case to his court.

But when Mrs. Mussey went to Rockville, Maryland, to present a case before the probate court, the judge not only stared at her in surprise but exclaimed before the assembled attorneys, "Well, this is the first time we've had a female lawyer appear here."

On one case Mrs. Mussey had to take a journey to a sparsely settled community south of Richmond, Va., to inspect some land. At her destination was a depot and a general store, and in the hope that she might find some means of conveyance to the property in question, she went to the store, introduced herself, and explained her business.

At once the storekeeper regarded her as a celebrity. Most assuredly he would get a conveyance for her as soon as possible and in the meantime, he made the most of the occasion. It was Christmas time, folks from the surrounding country were coming in to do their holiday shopping and each new arrival was ceremoniously presented to the "woman lawyer from Washington." A ferry landing was close by and a group of men and women stopped in the store on their way across the river to the estate of an Englishman who was entertaining at dinner that day.

No sooner had these people been introduced to Mrs. Mussey than they pounced upon her as a real find for the party. They insisted that she go with them, declaring their host would be delighted to have a woman lawyer as his guest. They would hardly accept her refusal, but she had to attend to business. That evening, as she waited for the train back to Washington, the visitors returned from across the river and told her that their host had been sadly disappointed because the woman lawyer had not come to his dinner.

She began to get used to being a phenomenon. Yet she was hardly prepared for the reception given her in the Dismal Swamp region where she had a case involving damages against the government for property which the owner, a northern man, claimed had been burned by northern troops during the Civil War.

The government representative in the case was General Edgar Allen, United States Attorney for the southern district of Virginia, with offices in Norfolk. Mrs. Mussey had known him and his family for many years, and she and the General set forth together from Norfolk for the little town where the case was to be heard.

Railroad service ended at a small station ten miles from the town and the rest of the journey had to be made by horse and gig across Dismal Swamp. But General Allen and Mrs. Mussey found when they got off the train, late that evening, that no conveyance would be available before morning.

They must find a place to stay for the night. It was a desolate, thinly settled region, however, and the stationmaster had no suggestions to offer, but while they were discussing the matter a youngster appeared and said that "Mam," who had a house up on the hill and boarded some bridge builders, might have a place for the travelers.

They went to Mam's house, and General Allen explained the situation, told the woman that he and Mrs. Mussey were lawyers and that the latter was from Washington, D. C.

And Mam, staring at Mrs. Mussey in unconcealed wonder, heartily agreed to provide sleeping quarters. She escorted the new arrivals to the sitting room and introduced them to a group of men and women sitting about the fireplace. "She's a woman lawyer from Washington," announced Mam with the air of one who has made the discovery of a lifetime.

Immediately all conversation ceased, both men and women devoting themselves to scrutinizing Mrs. Mussey. It made her uncomfortable, and presently, being weary from her journey, she asked to be shown to her room.

A bed stood in one corner of the sitting room and Mam said to the company, "You all get out of here. She wants to go to bed and she sleeps here."

The men and the women left the room but the women returned immediately to watch the woman lawyer undress. They were especially interested in her "city" underwear, as they called it, and wanted to know how much it cost.

The next morning they followed her about, never leaving her out of their sight until the gig arrived to take her and General Allen across the swamp.

And no sooner had they reached their destination and set about their business than word passed about that a woman lawyer was in town and the populace turned out to stare. They watched from windows, gathered in front of the stores, peeped from behind tree boxes, and peered around corners to get a look at her as she went down the street. General Allen, walking with her, declared he had never had so much attention in his life.

At the hotel where they ate noon dinner, Mrs. Mussey was kept under close surveillance. It may have been that her hosts feared that a woman who had taken a "man's" profession would as like as not expect all the privileges given a man. And sure enough, as soon as dinner was finished, Mrs. Mussey started with General Allen toward the hotel veranda to sit in the warm fall sunshine for a while.

But an attendant rushed after her and exclaimed, "You all don't go out there." Women were not allowed to sit on the hotel veranda and Mrs. Mussey had to content herself with a small and stuffy ladies' parlor.

When they went to the notary's office where the case was to be heard, the notary apologized profusely because he had no rocking chair for the "lady lawyer." He really had intended to go to the furniture store to get one, he said, but had been so busy he had not got round to it. The office, however, had been newly scrubbed and was still wet and shining for her benefit.

As soon as all questioning of the witnesses was finished, General Allen and Mrs. Mussey left the village, driving off amidst the stares of all those citizens who had got word in time to be at hand for the departure.

In 1896, three years after her admission to the bar, Mrs. Mussey was admitted to practice before the Supreme Court of the United States, the thirteenth woman to achieve this honor. It had been nearly twenty-seven years since her first visit to the court and she was no longer awed by its dignity and solemnity. She was merely taking another step in her advancement as a lawyer.

But the clerk of the court said, "That's hard, to be the thirteenth woman."

"No, indeed," laughed Mrs. Mussey. "Thirteen is my lucky number. I was born on the thirteenth."

In 1897 she was admitted to practice before the United States Court of Claims, the fourth woman to receive that recognition, and in 1900 as an associate of Robert D. Benedict, of New York City, she had her first case before the Supreme Court of the United States.

This was a suit against the government brought by an appointee who in accordance with a common practice of the times, had been permitted to hold two offices while he received but one salary. At a change in administration this appointee had been dropped and he sued for the additional salary.

Mrs. Mussey helped in the preparation of the brief but Mr. Benedict, as senior counsel, gave the oral argument and they won a full judgment for the plaintiff, an important decree because it resulted in new legislation regarding government appointees and salaries.

This was the beginning of a long and successful practice for Mrs. Mussey before the bar of the United States Supreme Court. But she was reaching out now beyond the practice of law.

CHAPTER XI

A DISCOVERY

Mrs. Mussey had many divorce cases. A large number of them came from men but still more of them were from women, and this practice brought revelations. Women, she found, were suffering the most shocking injustices because of the prevailing marriage laws. Not only did women bring their own marital troubles to Mrs. Mussey but her friends and acquaintances were continually informing her of appalling conditions that had come under their observation.

One case brought to her attention was a startling example of what went on under the District code. A little girl pupil had come to kindergarten in great distress because a strange man had appeared at her home, had claimed to be her father, and had forced her mother to take him in. The teacher investigated, learned that the man was the child's father, but that two years before he had deserted her and her mother who shortly afterward gave birth to a second child. Following this, the mother furnished the entire support for herself and her two children. Then, suddenly, the father returned and, through threats to take the children away from his wife, forced her to live with him and provide for him.

The children belonged to him. Though he had not seen the baby until it was nearly two years old, had never done anything toward its care and support, it was actually his under the law and he had a legal right to take it away from its mother.

The laws of the thirteen colonies and subsequently those of the District of Columbia had been derived from the old English common law which gave the father absolute right to the child born in wedlock. If he so desired, the father could will away his child even before it was born.

Numerous men, unwilling to work, took advantage of the rights the law gave them and, under threat to take away minor children, forced their wives to support them.

Men had still other legal advantages. A wife's earnings belonged to her husband. Even if a married woman had a separate estate by gift or inheritance the earnings from such property or business were lawfully her husband's. Also if a woman joined her husband in a deed of trust, encumbering real estate in his name, she lost her dower rights.

Thoroughly aroused by these legal discriminations against women, Mrs. Mussey in the fall of 1895 began a crusade to change the laws. She went first to a meeting of the District Federation of Women's Clubs, where she gave an enlightening talk on the District of Columbia code.

The Federation at once appointed a legislative committee, with Mrs. Mussey as chairman, Miss Emma Gillett, Mrs. Mary S. Lockwood, Mrs. Lucia Blount, and Mrs. Elliott Coues, to take action to remedy these evils. Mrs. Mussey and Miss Gillett, who was also an attorney, sought the help of Judge David Brewer, Associate Justice of the United States Supreme Court, who was from Kansas and who had been instrumental in freeing women of that state from legal injustices.

Judge Brewer gave his whole-hearted assistance, and Mrs. Mussey drafted a bill covering the main inequalities of the law, giving the mother the same rights as the father in the child, giving the married woman the right to her own earnings, and safeguarding her dower rights.

Under the existing law, men, too, suffered hardships. When a man married he became legally responsible for any debts his wife had contracted before marriage. The new bill was drawn to remove this discrimination.

Mrs. Mussey sent her bill to Senator McMillan, of Michigan, who was chairman of the District committee, and he introduced it and gave it his active support. Afterward it was referred to a sub-committee and later to the District Commissioners who sent it to the District Bar Association, and one of their number, J. J. Darlington, was appointed to confer with Mrs. Mussey.

In general he approved the bill, and after a few changes it was returned to the sub-committee of the Senate. The next problem was to get the support of as many senators as possible and Mrs. Mussey knew this would require the concerted efforts of the club women of Washington.

Night after night she went to meetings, explained the new measure, urged women to give it their support and to interview Senators in its behalf. Organizations responded quickly and sent delegations to the Capitol to lobby for the bill.

Mrs. Mussey, herself, lost no opportunity to talk to senators on the subject. One day she happened to be on the same elevator with Senator Francis E. Warren, of Wyoming, and she immediately launched forth upon the merits of her bill.

But Senator Warren exclaimed, "Don't waste your time on me. I believe in your bill, but if I didn't I'd have to vote for it because I'm here through women's votes." Wyoming had been admitted as a state with full suffrage for women, the first state in the Union to grant woman suffrage.

Few senators, however, gave consideration to women constituents because women in general did not have the vote and there were senators who firmly believed that the father should be the sole guardian of the children. Objection to the bill was strong, especially in the sub-committee which had charge of it. The chairman, himself, Senator Faulkner, of West Virginia, opposed it. The sub-committee had reached a deadlock on the matter and to break this, three additional members were appointed.

Senator Gallingher, of New Hampshire, who was interested in the measure, informed Mrs. Mussey of the new appointees and she made haste to interview them. One senator was from Kansas and he approved the bill, another was from Virginia and he promised favorable action. That gave her a majority, but Mr. Faulkner remained hostile and his attitude was of grave concern to Mrs. Mussey and her committee.

One section of the bill, however, won the commendation of congressmen and men in general. It was the clause eliminating the husband's responsibility for his wife's prenuptial debts. That was something the men could understand and appreciate and prospective bridegrooms were waylaying congressmen in an effort to get favorable and speedy action on this bill. Prospective wives, too, joined in the campaign.

One day an exceedingly good looking and attractively dressed widow came to Mrs. Mussey's office and offered her services. Glad to get all available assistance, Mrs. Mussey gave the young woman a list of senators to interview.

Later, Mrs. Mussey learned that the widow was engaged to marry a Washington business man, that a judgment of twenty thousand dollars was held against her, and in order to prevent the prospective husband from becoming liable for this debt, the couple had postponed their marriage and were working tirelessly to get the Mussey bill passed.

But the proposed measure received its greatest impetus from a sensational case that came up in a District court. As a rule it was the women of the poorer classes who suffered from the injustices of the law and such cases were given little or no publicity, but shortly after Mrs. Mussey had made her plans to amend the law, a striking illustration of its needs was brought to public attention.

A prominent society man and former naval officer died and left a will in which he gave his two little daughters to his sister. The mother of the children, a woman of wealth who had furnished the entire support for her two little girls, contested the will, and the ensuing battle stirred all Washington. Even senators were aroused, and Senator William E. Chandler, of New Hampshire, heatedly denounced a law that permitted a father to will a child away from its mother. The case came at an opportune time and it won converts to the new bill that no amount of talking could have done.

Yet Senator Faulkner, chairman of the sub-committee in charge of the measure, showed no sign of relenting in its favor. Mrs. Mussey and Mrs. Blount went to see him to make a final plea in its behalf. They stressed the mother's right to her child.

But Senator Faulkner seemed adamant. "Men have a great deal more sense than women," he said, "and they should have the right to say what shall be done with the children."

"Yes," cried Mrs. Mussey caustically, "when a woman is left a widow with small children she goes to work to support them, but when a man is left with small children he marries a young woman as soon as possible."

At that the senator chuckled. Then some one called for him and he left, still chuckling. But Mrs. Blount turned upon Mrs. Mussey sharply. "Now, you've done it," she exclaimed. "That's just what Senator Faulkner did, married a young girl when he was left with small children."

Mrs. Mussey was aghast. She had not known about the senator's marriage. Had she jeopardized the chances of her bill, she wondered miserably? But nothing could be done but await the outcome.

In the end Senator Faulkner was quite fair in his treatment, was responsible, in fact, for speeding up action on the measure. It passed the Senate and went to the House.

After certain minor changes to perfect the wording, it was scheduled to come up on the next District day, but action on it was postponed until the following District day and Mrs. Mussey learned that in the interim the handsome widow and the business man who had been so interested in the bill, fairly hounded the congressmen to urge its passage so that they would not have to postpone their marriage again.

No difficulty was encountered in the House, the measure was passed without debate, and was signed by the President, Grover Cleveland, June 1, 1896.

Washington, D. C., had no kindergartens except a few conducted by benevolent societies for the benefit of underprivileged children. Though kindergartens had gained some favor in the larger cities of the country as early as 1874 and as the years passed were being established in connection with public school systems, Washington had no part in this advancement.

For years the School Board had been asking for an appropriation of $12,000 for kindergartens but Congress regarded this as an extravagance, and every year the item was cut from the appropriation bill. At last, in 1898, wholly out of patience, the Superintendent of Schools, W. B. Powell, sought Mrs. Mussey's assistance. She was chairman of the Legislative Committee of the District Federation of Women's Clubs and had offered her services for school legislation.

Having no knowledge of kindergartens, Mrs. Mussey went to William T. Harris, Commissioner of Education, to get information on the subject. He said he would be glad to help her, on one condition. She must promise not to use his name in connection with the information he gave her. "For if you tell those congressmen on the District Committee that you've been to see me," Mr. Harris declared, "they will say at once, 'Oh! that's just another of Harris' cranky notions.' "

When she had obtained all the facts available, Mrs. Mussey went to see Senator Allison, of Iowa, chairman of the appropriation committee, with whom she was well acquainted. He advised her to prepare a brief on kindergartens and promised her a hearing before the sub-committee of the District. But he warned her that the committee was a hard one to deal with and the clerk of the committee was discouraging, too. "You can't make any headway with those men," he told Mrs. Mussey.

But she prepared her brief with care and had copies printed to give to each senator on the committee. Her heart sank, however, when she saw the men assembled to hear her arguments. Besides Senator Allison, there was Senator Gorman, of Maryland; Senator Quay, of Pennsylvania, and Senator Cullom, of Illinois, all of them influential men of the Senate. How was she to interest them in kindergartens?

But she began as impressively as possible, "Gentlemen, the dearest thing in the world to a woman is a child."

Immediately Senator Quay responded, "And so it is to a man, too."

That seemed hopeful, Mrs. Mussey thought, and she proceeded to explain the work of kindergartens, their value in giving the child associations with others of its own age, their training in preparation for the grade school work, and their need in particular for underprivileged children. She talked for ten minutes and when she had finished the senators asked for copies of her statement. It was the first time anyone had made an effort to show them why kindergartens were needed, and as a result the item for kindergartens was put into the appropriation bill.

Greater difficulty was encountered in the House, however, for the chairman of the conferees, a confirmed bachelor from New England, was totally opposed to using taxpayers' money for kindergartens. "Kindergartens should be left in the hands of charity," he said. "If you take them away there will be nothing left for charity to do. Besides, if we allow you $12,000 now, you'll be coming around for more later."

"We most assuredly will," agreed Mrs. Mussey, "for $12,000 is a mere drop in the bucket so far as needs are concerned."

Mrs. Mussey asked friends to call upon this congressman, but he would not promise to help. When the appropriations bill was approved, June 30, 1898, however, the item for kindergartens was included and the following year sixteen kindergartens, eight for white children and eight for colored children, were established.

Washington had many saloons, so many that they had become a serious problem and a law was enacted providing for a decrease of one hundred saloons annually. This was done by refusing licenses to disorderly establishments and by limiting the number of saloons in certain sections. There was a general feeling that it was inadvisable to close more than one hundred saloons at a time because of the lack of other occupations to absorb the men thus thrown out of work.

Saloonkeepers and liquor interests, of course, fought the closing of even one hundred saloons, and heated battles were fought between them and the citizenry. Sometimes a group of people would succeed in having a disorderly place closed only to find it opened again the next year as disorderly as ever.

When the Musseys moved to K Street near the intersection of Pennsylvania Avenue and Twenty-first Street, there were three saloons on the corners, and one of them was exceedingly disreputable. With saloons so numerous, competition was keen, and this saloon, in order to build up its business, displayed obscene pictures in its windows to attract the young men and boys of the neighborhood.

Mothers came to Mrs. Mussey and complained that their boys had been enticed into this saloon and they begged her to do something. Mrs. Mussey, herself, had seen some of the ribald bids for customers because she had to pass this saloon on her way to her office. She appeared before the Excise Board, put up a vigorous fight against the renewal of its license, and at last succeeded in having the saloon closed.

The saloonkeeper bitterly resented her action and hated her because of it. When General Mussey died, the saloonkeeper taunted her. He still remained on his premises, and as she passed on her way to her law office, he called after her, "Good enough for you that you lost your husband. You closed my saloon."

But the next year the Excise Board renewed the license for this saloon and it continued as disorderly as before. One Christmas Eve, as Mrs. Mussey was passing, a drunken man was thrown out in the snow. She met a policeman directly afterward and told him of the incident, but he showed no sign of doing anything. She took the matter up with the Excise Board, but at the hearing the policeman said he had not seen the man thrown out so he could do nothing. All efforts to have the saloon closed at this time were unavailing.

Often Mrs. Mussey appeared before committees of Congress in an effort to get more drastic action against disreputable saloons, but the saloon question was frequently lost in the press of other legislation for the District. Once she went to Champ Clark, Speaker of the House, to get his assistance in putting through the yearly reduction in saloons, but Mr. Clark said, "Mrs. Mussey, there's no use trying to do anything until you have the vote in the District of Columbia."

CHAPTER XII

FOUNDING A LAW SCHOOL

It was not a new thing, according to history, for women to take an active part in the practice of law. A woman had even been a judge.

More than a thousand years before Christ, Deborah, the prophetess, judged the children of Israel. Wisely, too, for freeing Israel from its oppressors, she guided it through forty years of peace. Nor did the Israelites, so far as the records show, regard it as unusual for a woman to be a judge. They evidently accepted Deborah as they accepted any other great leader.

But to the ancient Romans women who engaged in legal practice seemed abnormal beings. The historian Maximus Valerius referred to them as "those women whom the conditions of their sex and the garments of modesty could not hinder from appearing and speaking in public courts of judicature."

One of "those women" was Amasia Sentia who, according to Maximus Valerius, "being guilty before a great concourse of people, pleaded her own cause; and observing all the parts and elegancies of a true defense not only diligently but stoutly, was acquitted in her first action by the sentence of all. And because that under the shape of a woman, she carried a manly resolution, they called her Androgynon." In other words, they believed that to achieve this success, Amasia Sentia must be half man.

Another Roman woman who won a legal victory was Hortensia, the daughter of Q. Hortensius, and the historian wrote of her, "when the order of matrons was too heavily taxed by the triumvirs, and that none of the men durst undertake to speak in their behalfs, she pleaded the matrons' cause; not only with boldness but success. For the image of her father's eloquence obtained that the greater part of the imposition was remitted." Once again man was given a share in the victory.

But he wanted no credit for the legal activities of Afrania, the wife of Licinius Buccio, the senator. Being extremely troubled with lawsuits, Afrania always pleaded for herself before the praetor, according to Valerius, "not that she wanted advocates, but because she abounded in impudence. So that with the perpetual vexing of the tribunal with her bawling, to which the court was unaccustomed, she grew to be a noted example of female Calumnie. So that the name Afrania was given to all contentious women."

It is quite likely that the Romans seized upon Afrania as an argument against women in the practice of law and contended with more determination than ever that they should not take part in this profession because of the "conditions of their sex." At least that became the treasured, the all-embracing argument against women in the law, and man clung to it down through the centuries.

But even so, women scaled the barriers now and then to renown at the bar. In 1498 Joan of Arc, untutored peasant girl of sixteen, confronted with a false charge of having promised to marry a certain young man and brought before the ecclesiastical court at Toul for an accounting, pleaded her own cause with such ingeniousness that she confounded the young man in question as well as all his witnesses, and the case was thrown out of court.

A little later while she was endeavoring to rally the armies of France and lead an attack upon the English oppressors, she was questioned by the illustrious doctors of the University of Poitiers on the soundness of her piety. And by the simplicity and directness of her defense she won a sweeping victory which resulted in her being proclaimed by the King as general-in-chief of the armies of France.

Even at the great trial in Rouen, following her capture by the enemy, the Maid of Orleans, alone and unaided, set at naught the wit and learning of sixty-two trained men, and only through the basest treachery did they finally triumph over her and send her to the stake.

America, itself, early in the history of the colonies, had a woman who practiced law. Mistress Margaret Brent came to Maryland in 1638 and acted as attorney for Lord Baltimore and Gov. Leonard Calvert. Mistress Brent won a reputation for sagacity and good sense among the Maryland assemblymen, and when Lord Baltimore reprimanded her for being too aggressive in certain government activities, the assemblymen rallied to her support and let it be known to his Lordship that she was the "ablest man among them."

However, they, too, disapproved when she grew so bold as to ask for the vote, the first woman in the country to demand the right of suffrage. Perhaps the only reason Mistress Brent was allowed to plead before the Maryland courts was because the new colony had as yet enacted no regulations regarding admission to the bar. For as soon as the men got round to making a law about it, they promptly excluded women from the practice of this profession.

Not until more than two hundred years later was a woman duly licensed to practice law in the United States. Iowa, the first state in the Union to grant a woman formal admission to the bar, ushered in a new era, and in another quarter of a century women began to gain a foothold in the law.

But prejudice against them persisted. In the District of Columbia a most unique and paradoxical condition prevailed. Women were admitted to practice before all the courts of the District, the Supreme Court of the United States, and all executive departments, yet at the same time they were denied admission to all the law schools for white persons. But the District had one school that accepted women in its law classes—Howard University—a school for Negroes. And white women studied law there.

For some women, however, it was not expedient to attend this school, and in their search for a legal education they were seriously handicapped. One such young woman was Miss Delia Sheldon Jackson, daughter of the Rev. Sheldon Jackson, wealthy patron of education among the Alaskan Indians. Since he had no sons, the Rev. Mr. Jackson wished to train one of his daughters to manage his fortune and keep it in trust for educational work, and it was Miss Delia who showed a liking and aptitude for this work.

To prepare herself fully for the task, Miss Jackson wanted to study law but the white law schools refused admission to her just as they had to other women. There were several women practicing law in Washington, however, and Miss Jackson, at the suggestion of General John Eaton, former Commissioner of Education, went to Ellen Spencer Mussey and asked permission to read law in her office.

Mrs. Mussey refused the request. She had been a member of the bar less than three years, she was sufficiently occupied with building up a clientele, and she felt she had neither the time nor the energy for the additional responsibility of a law student.

But Miss Jackson was insistent. So was her father, who came again and again to see Mrs. Mussey. And General Eaton, too, urged her consent. At last Mrs. Mussey said that if there were two other young women interested in studying law, she would try to get the assistance of Miss Emma Gillett and form a law class. Miss Gillett was in active practice, had studied law under Mrs. Belva Lockwood, first woman of the law in Washington, and later, Miss Gillett had been graduated from Howard University, the school for Negroes.

Mrs. Mussey did not believe that in all Washington two other young women could be found who wanted an education in the law and accordingly she gave the matter no further thought. But in a surprisingly short time Mrs. Nanette B. Paul and Miss Helen Malcolm came to add their pleas to those of Miss Jackson, and Mrs. Mussey had to fulfill her promise. Miss Gillett agreed to give her assistance, and on the afternoon of February 1, 1896, the Women's Law Class of three students met for the first time. Mrs. Mussey instructed them in constitutional law and Miss Gillett taught the common law as stated by Blackstone.

Classes continued for four months, examinations were held in May, and students and teachers celebrated with a luncheon at the home of Miss Malcolm. That was the end of the Women's Law Class, or so Mrs. Mussey thought, hopefully. She was determined now to give her entire time to her practice.

But in the fall, the young women were back again, and with them were still other women, Mrs. Emma Reba Bailey, Mrs. Margaret Lohr, Miss Caroline Griesheimer, and Miss Flora Raymond, all eager for instruction in the law. Mrs. Mussey had not the heart to refuse them, and she and Miss Gillett began at this time to give instruction in the regular subjects taught in law schools. They scheduled their classes in the evening instead of the afternoon, to accommodate certain of the women who were employed in government offices.

This proved a heavy program for the two instructors and they sought additional help among the men of the bar. W. J. Newton, with whom Miss Gillett was associated in the practice of law, became one of the regular teachers, and lectures were given by Seth Shepard, Associate Justice of the Court of Appeals, and William C. Robinson, Dean of the Law School at Catholic University, who had been a classmate of General Mussey at Dartmouth.

By 1898, six young women were ready for the senior year's work in law. But Mrs. Mussey and Miss Gillett did not wish to establish a college, so they went to the President of Columbian College (later George Washington University) and asked that the six young women be admitted to that school for their final work in law. The matter was referred to the Board of Trustees and deliberated. Then, in spite of the fact that women were admitted to the bar in all the courts of the District, in spite of the fact that the six women had qualified throughout the preliminary law study, the Board refused them admission. Mrs. Mussey was told that conservative members still insisted that women had not the mentality for law.

Like their ancient Roman brothers, the trustees apparently believed that women were incapacitated by the "conditions of their sex" and under no circumstances was this cherished theory to be subjected to the rigors of a practical test. Yet something had to be done about these six young women law students. Mrs. Mussey and Miss Gillett discussed the problem with leading members of the bar.

"Start a law school of your own," was the advice given.

That seemed a serious step and Mrs. Mussey was wary. She would find out first about the status of women in the law schools where they were admitted. She wrote to the heads of several law schools.

The dean of the department of law at the University of Michigan replied, "Women who have attended the law school have compared favorably in matters of scholarship with men." Another dean wrote, "We discover no difference in the capacity of the sexes to apprehend and apply legal principles." From the secretary of still another school came the assurance that "the women who have attended our school have all been very bright students and have made excellent records."

With such high recommendations of women as law students, Mrs. Mussey and Miss Gillett felt impelled to found a law school, and on April 9, 1898, the Washington College of Law was incorporated.

It was the first law school in the world to be established primarily for women. But it was co-educational. To the founders it seemed both just and wise to admit men on the same terms as women. Also a three-year course was established at once though certain other law schools were still confined to two-year courses.

And the college chose for its dean, not a man as law schools had done for centuries, but a woman, Ellen Spencer Mussey, the first woman in the world to be dean of a law school.

A strange and precarious concern, this law college was. For it was founded without a dollar of endowment or donated fund. It must, therefore, depend almost entirely upon the members of the bar for its support. But Mrs. Mussey felt no hesitancy in asking assistance, and judges, lawyers, and professors gladly promised their services as instructors without any thought of pay. They served on the Board of Trustees, too.

When Mrs. Mussey asked Edward F. Bingham, Chief Justice of the District Supreme Court, if he would serve as a member of the Board, he said, "Of course I will." Judge Bingham was elected president; Mrs. Cecelia Sherman, wife of Senator Sherman, vice-president; and other members were Judge Charles B. Howry, of the Court of Claims; Mrs. J. Ellen Foster, practicing attorney and pioneer woman political speaker; W. J. Newton, Miss Gillett, and Mrs. Mussey.

That fall Mrs. Mussey and Miss Gillett prepared enthusiastically for the first fall opening of their college. It was to be somewhat of a reception, with a lecture by Miss Gillett. Printed invitations were sent out, and the college heads expected a large attendance.

But the appointed hour arrived and the guests were distressingly few. Apparently this law school for women had aroused very little interest. The minutes ticked by. Yet no one else came. Bravely, Miss Gillett began her lecture.

There was still hope that others might come, however, and Mrs. Mussey, in order that she might greet them, went outside and closed the door behind her to shut out any disturbing noises. She was just in time.

Several newspaper reporters were coming up the steps. The opening of a law school for women, a law school with a woman as dean—this was news. With quick decision, Mrs. Mussey placed herself between the door and the reporters. Under no circumstances must they find out what a failure the meeting was.

They plied her with questions about the school, the prospective students, and the evening's program. They asked if there was a good crowd present. And though Miss Gillett was lecturing to an almost empty hall, Mrs. Mussey told the reporters that the attendance was very good, assuring herself inwardly that those who had come must indeed be very good or they would not have come. She felt greatly relieved when at last the reporters left. And the write-ups in the papers next day were much more encouraging than the meeting had been.

But most of the former students registered for work that fall and there were a few new ones. The financial outlook, though, was depressing. Tuition was fifty dollars a year, purposely made lower than in other law schools because this was a school primarily for women, and women, even though they did the same work as men, seldom received the same pay. As a result there was not only no money to pay instructors but there was not enough money for other expenses.

To help out Mrs. Mussey gave the use of her private office and the services of her stenographer for college business, yet even then it was difficult to make ends meet. The worry of this venture and the hours of teaching, along with her own law practice, seemed more than she could bear, and sometimes at the end of an arduous day she longed for the relief that would be hers if the college should fail.

But somehow, it buffeted through that first year and achieved a triumph, its first commencement held May 31, 1899. All six young women for whose benefit the college had been founded, Mrs. Emma Reba Bailey, of Georgia; Miss Caroline Griesheimer, of Ohio; Miss Delia Sheldon Jackson and Mrs. Margaret Lohr, of the District of Columbia; Miss Helen Malcolm, of Virginia, and Miss Flora Raymond, of New York, had successfully completed the three-year course. Graduates, undergraduates, and faculty members beamed with pride.

Surely it was a time for rejoicing, an occasion to inspire whole-hearted praise and encouragement, yet the prejudice and skepticism against women of the law forced an inning even at this commencement.

The speaker of the evening was a former congressman from South Carolina who was practicing law in the District of Columbia. Mrs. Mussey had had nothing to do with his selection and she did not know why he had been chosen for this event, but he was a handsome man and he looked well on the platform.

Ellen Spencer Mussey as Dean of the law school, 1899.

He had not talked long, however, before he made it plain that he was very doubtful about women's ability in the law. In fact, he seemed to be against the whole advancement of women and he declared pointedly that the old-time woman was good enough for him.

At this Dean Mussey's dark eyes flashed fire, and Justice Seth Shepard, who was sitting on the platform, noted it and chuckled in anticipation.

When the speaker had finished, Mrs. Mussey thanked him for his talk. "But it is very evident," she exclaimed, "that the honorable Mr. ——— is badly in need of information as to why women are studying law. I never had any doubts that the old-time woman was good enough for any man. In fact, she was too good, and the present-day woman is not studying law to be good enough for some man but to have the opportunities that men have."

Prejudice, always it was cropping up. Financial odds, too, seemed overwhelming. Mrs. Mussey wondered how long a law school such as this could survive.

Chapter XIII

THE RED CROSS *vs.* RED TAPE

Mrs. Mussey was in excellent health and her small figure was beginning to show the plumpness of middle age. It wrought havoc in her wardrobe, and in the spring of 1898 she set aside one hundred fifty dollars to buy new clothes.

Then she was asked to go as a delegate to the convention of the General Federation of Women's Clubs, to be held in Denver. This was an opportunity to see the west, and all the glowing dreams of her girlhood days came trooping back at the prospect. But she had to have money for this sort of journey and it was far from plentiful.

There was the clothes fund, however, and after all what were new clothes compared to the adventures of a trip west? She went to Denver.

But it took careful planning for one hundred fifty dollars would permit few luxuries. She did not stop at hotels and fine restaurants. She patronized rooming houses and cheap little restaurants. And she had to confine Pullman comforts to nighttime riding. Every morning she went back to the day coach. But this frugality did not trouble her. She was seeing the west.

It irked her, though, to be limited to the small patches of scenery available from the day coach windows. She wanted a sweeping panorama of this glorious west. So, she went outside and sat on the car steps. She was avid to see the Royal Gorge and long before the train had reached this scenic spot she had settled herself at her usual vantage point.

But just as the train entered the gorge, a man came out on the platform and said, "Madam will you let me step down in front of you?"

"Indeed, I won't!" retorted Mrs. Mussey. "I've been holding this place for a long time and I don't intend to give it up now."

Then he informed her that he was the engineer who had built the railroad through the gorge and if she would at least let him come down beside her, he would tell her about it.

That seemed a bargain, and through smoke and showers of cinders the law school dean and the engineer viewed the magnificent scenery of the Royal Gorge.

Denver churches turned their Sunday meetings over to the women of the convention, and Mrs. Mussey was assigned to the Presbyterian church. From its lofty pulpit she delivered what she liked to call her first "sermon."

When she returned to Washington she plunged immediately into relief work. For the country was at war with Spain.

Mrs. Mussey was attorney and executive committee member of the Red Cross, a new and still rather untried organization in the United States. General Mussey had been its first counsel. He and Miss Clara Barton, founder of the Red Cross in the United States, had become acquainted back in the days following the Civil War when he had been military secretary to President Johnson.

Many people sought interviews with President Johnson and among them was a dark slender woman with piercing black eyes who came day after day, waited long hours, and was always turned away without seeing the President. Yet the next day she was sure to be back again. At last, struck by her persistence, General Mussey asked if he might be of some assistance, and the woman, who was Miss Clara Barton, explained her project.

Countless families did not know where their soldier dead had been buried during the Civil War, and Miss Barton, who had conducted relief work among the wounded and dying, had succeeded in getting the names and burial places of hundreds of soldiers. To facilitate giving this information to their families, she sought the aid of the President.

General Mussey suggested placing in postoffices throughout the country printed lists of the soldiers' names and burial places and talked the matter over with President Johnson, who gave it his approval.

Miss Barton had devoted herself so tirelessly to relief work during the war and following it that her health was broken, and in 1869, upon the advice of her physician, she went to Europe for a rest. While in Geneva she learned of the Red Cross Treaty, drawn up at an international convention in that city in 1864, to provide for the proper care of sick and injured soldiers during time of war, and at once Miss Barton became one of its enthusiastic advocates.

She was at the front during the Franco-Prussian war, the first conflict to follow the signing of the treaty, and she saw the amazing results of relief work that was authorized and organized. Compared to it, relief such as had been given during the Civil War seemed clumsy and ineffectual, and Miss Barton was eager to have her own country sign the Red Cross Treaty.

Many European and South American nations had signed the treaty, and the United States had been urged to do likewise, but the country had remained aloof, fearful of international entanglements. Miss Barton, therefore, set herself the task of winning the country's approval.

But not until Garfield's administration was the treaty given favorable consideration. It was finally signed in March, 1882, by President Chester A. Arthur.

In anticipation of this, Miss Barton on May 21, 1881, had organized a National Society of the Red Cross in Washington, D. C. She had asked General Mussey to act as the Society's attorney, and he and Mrs. Mussey had been charter members. Miss Barton also organized a local Red Cross Society at Dansville, N. Y., her home town. But few other societies came into being at this time, and the Red Cross, though it gave relief following such disasters as the Michigan forest fires, Mississippi floods, and other calamities, remained rather local in its scope. What its value might be in a national crisis was still to be proved, but the crucial test came during the Spanish-American War.

The Red Cross at this time faced the problem not only of raising money, gathering and distributing supplies of medicine, food, and clothing, and providing physicians and nurses, but of winning the coöperation of the military authorities so that relief work could be carried on.

This was a task. For certain military officials had no use for the Red Cross. They were opposed to any kind of interference. This attitude was evident in a report by Mr. B. H. Warner, chairman of the executive committee of the Red Cross at Washington, which had charge of relief work in nearby camps, including Camp Alger and Fort Myer. Mr. Warner recorded, "I found Colonel Girard (of Camp Alger) exceedingly busy and apparently very sanguine as to the ability of the Government to meet all the demands that might be made by every department of the army. . . . I was thoroughly impressed with the fact that he considered men who had received the regular army education, thoroughly competent to meet the situation, and that all supplies could be had as soon as needed; and that he did not want too many comforts for sick men, so as to unfit them for the hardships of war."

In the same report: "Surgeons at the hospitals seemed to be timid about asking the Government for supplies. The Surgeon-in-Chief seemed to think that the soldiers who were taken sick should be treated in such a manner as would inure them to the hardships of camp and the life of a soldier. When spoken to on this subject, this official said, 'These men must understand that war is not play.' "

Plainly it was not. Conditions at the Washington camps were intolerable. Hundreds of soldiers, stricken with fever, were being brought up from the south, yet facilities for their care were entirely inadequate. Hospitals were overflowing, food was wretched, the heat was intense, and scores of men were dying.

At Fort Myer across the Potomac, nearly four hundred men were ill with typhoid fever, but the camp was prepared to care for no more than thirty patients. It was impossible to feed the men properly, particularly those who were convalescing, and the diet of convalescents was considered paramount.

Word of the extreme privation and suffering came to the Red Cross. It was prepared to provide diet kitchens for just such emergencies and Mrs. Mussey had been put in charge of this work. With her assistant, Mrs. J. A. T. Hull, wife of Congressman Hull, of Iowa, she planned to establish a diet kitchen at Fort Myer.

But the Surgeon-General, George M. Sternberg, in command of the army medical service, was opposed to assistance from the Red Cross, and no relief could be given without authority. Mrs. Mussey must find a way to get this authority. She sought the aid of Corporal James Tanner, veteran of the Civil War and a member of the G. A. R. Corporal Tanner had received such severe wounds in the second battle of Bull Run that both his legs had had to be amputated on the battlefield, under fire, and he could understand the value of relief work. He arranged an interview for Mrs. Mussey with a high authority, General R. A. Alger, the Secretary of War, himself.

General Alger was reasonable. He gave Mrs. Mussey a written order authorizing the establishment of diet kitchens at the camps. Thus armed and accompanied by Mrs. Hull, Mrs. Mussey went to Surgeon-General Sternberg to discuss plans for a diet kitchen at Fort Myer.

"But we don't need it," protested the General emphatically.

"We know conditions," insisted Mrs. Mussey. "You do need it and I have a written order." He had to comply, and he telephoned Major Davis, in charge at Fort Myer, concerning the order from the Secretary of War.

Major Davis, too, was opposed to the Red Cross and he yielded with poor grace to the Secretary's order. When Mrs. Mussey asked if he had a building that she might use as a diet kitchen he replied with a thunderous "No."

"Very well," replied Mrs. Mussey, "you have plenty of land. We'll put up a building."

Major Davis laughed derisively, "By the time you put up a building, you won't need it."

But he did not know the Red Cross. Within ten days the building, a temporary structure costing $350, was completed, furnished, and actually in operation as a diet kitchen. Dr. Mary Greene, of Cincinnati, Ohio, President of the National Household Economics Association, was put in charge.

The sick men were given beef, mutton, and chicken broth, made fresh daily from the best meats obtainable. They were provided with custards, blanc-mange, port and sherry wines. No money was spared in the purchase of food to repair the bodies wasted by fever. Even citrous fruits, expensive in summer, were supplied. There was ice cream, too.

Officials of the regular army and the War Department were horrified at this extravagance. It was unheard of to treat soldiers in such a luxurious fashion, regardless of how ill they might be. Certain members of the local Red Cross voiced objections also. Surely, they contended, ice cream was an inordinate extravagance.

But some of the invalid soldiers had asked for ice cream. And these boys had given themselves to their country. Mrs. Mussey felt that a little ice cream was small return for such a sacrifice. Besides, a committee of wealthy subscribers to the Red Cross in New York who were supplying funds for this relief had adopted as their motto, "Never spare a dollar if you can save a man." Mrs. Mussey believed in taking the motto literally.

The Red Cross not only supplied the soldiers with food, delicacies, and medicine, but furnished clothing, mattresses, sheets, pillow cases, mosquito bar, and many other comforts. Physicians and nurses were enthusiastic in their praise of the relief work and they assured the Red Cross that the diet kitchens were invaluable in saving lives and hastening the recovery of the sick men.

In time the officials of the regular army began to see the value of the Red Cross. Mr. Warner said in his committee report, "It is gratifying to be able to state that whatever views the surgeons and other officials may have had as to the need of the Red Cross at the beginning of the war, at the close they joined with the private soldiers in testifying to its wonderful and efficient work."

Even Major Davis at Fort Myer, who had been so hostile at the beginning, expressed his appreciation of the relief work.

It was through sheer efficacy that the Red Cross won converts. Surgeons said, "It is easier to ask the Red Cross for supplies and they can be obtained sooner than by asking the Government as there is so much red tape and it takes so long to get everything."

Astonishing proof of this was encountered at Point Sheridan, Virginia. Sanitary conditions at this camp were appalling. Sick men were housed in tents close to excreta, flies were swarming, the heat was intense, and medicine was lacking. Men in charge told Mrs. Mussey that what they needed above all else was quinine. It had been ordered more than a month before from the War Department but it still had not arrived.

Mrs. Mussey said, "I'll have that quinine here within twenty-four hours." And the medicine was delivered the next morning. That was the Red Cross.

Not only did it win the favor of the army, but the recognition of the general public, and when the war ended it seemed an auspicious time for national incorporation. Miss Barton established headquarters at her home at Glen Echo on the Potomac above Washington, and there she and Mrs. Mussey prepared the articles of incorporation and drew up a bill to be introduced in Congress.

In their preparatory work they held many conferences with public officials, and one day they visited John Hay, Secretary of State. Miss Barton had made his acquaintance in the days of President Johnson's regime and she asked Mr. Hay if he remembered her.

"Yes," he replied, "I do remember you. I was lamentably young then. Now I am lamentably old."

The bill providing for national incorporation of the Red Cross was passed by Congress and became a law June 6, 1906. Reorganization followed, and Mrs. Mussey continued as counselor for the national society.

CHAPTER XIV

A JOURNEY TO EUROPE

With law school responsibilities, Red Cross work, and a rapidly increasing law practice, Mrs. Mussey's days were brimming. But in the midst of these activities, in the spring of 1900, she was invited to go to Europe as the guest of a client, Mrs. Wood, widow of Arthur B. Wood, who had been in the United States consular service and whose business affairs had been in the hands of General and Mrs. Mussey for years.

This was a golden opportunity for Mrs. Mussey and she longed to see Europe, but with so many pressing duties she felt that she dared not go. Mrs. Wood, however, was insistent, and Mrs. Mussey's family, her son, her daughter, and Miss Lizzie, or Miss Betty, as the young folks preferred to call her, urged acceptance of this remarkable invitation. And finally Mrs. Mussey yielded.

Her family was eager to hear of her travels, Miss Betty asking in particular for information about what people ate in foreign countries, so Mrs. Mussey wrote in detail of her experiences. Some of these letters were kept as a kind of diary of her journey.

Rotterdam, April 16, 1900.

My dear Folks at Home: We arrived at Antwerp early Easter Sunday morning and, after breakfast, went directly to the beautiful cathedral which was begun in the fourteenth century before America was discovered and finished in the sixteenth century. The tower is more than four hundred feet high, and the chimes consist of ninety-nine bells, all as sweet as possible.

We saw the wonderful pictures by Reubens. They were companion pieces, the Ascent and the Descent from the Cross, which are considered the finest, but I liked best the picture of the marriage feast with Christ performing the miracle of turning the water into wine. Every face in that stands out as if it were molded.

Later we went back for grand mass. Mrs. Wood got tired, and I had to go out with her. We sat on little dusty chairs for which a funny old woman collected a penny each. Then the beadle came around and took up a collection.

Mrs. Wood went to Brussels this morning but I came on here. I am alone but so far find no trouble for nearly everywhere there is some one who speaks English. It was a fine ride here ,and I had my first sight of the dikes and windmills of Holland. This town is all canals and rivers. So far I have not seen a single carriage but they have very funny little street cars drawn by one horse and there are many queer signs and advertisements. You see "Quaker Oats" everywhere.

I am so glad to be here at Easter time for the holiday brings the peasants into town in their gala attire. The headdresses are still just as you see them in pictures and a few of the women wear queer special things standing out at the sides of the eyes like the blinders on a horse.

Amsterdam, April 17, 1900.

It was a charming ride from Rotterdam this morning. We came through Delft, where the Delft ware is made, and The Hague, and past the bulb farms of Holland. There were great gardens of flowers, red, white, blue, pink, yellow, and purple. Some of the beds were one hundred feet square and other looked like a quilt pieced up.

The windmills are everywhere. The farms are divided by ditches into fields and everything for farm use is floated on boats on the ditches, and drawn by a man with a rope around his neck. The fields are very rich, and there are many families of little pigs. Pigs and sheep are the only animals I saw this morning in the country. In Rotterdam, I saw great droves of cattle being driven to the butcher. The city is all canals. Someone calls it the "Vulgar Venice." Just think, I am on the Zuyder Zee.

Today we went to Waterloo. It was a warm spring day, perfect for such an excursion. We met out there a funny little girl from Kentucky, traveling all by herself. She knew a great deal about books but about geography she was as ignorant as an infant. She was going to Paris and proposed to arrive there most any time of night and look up a nice cheap place in the Latin quarter. I gave her a little motherly advice, which she accepted sweetly. It made me so anxious to see her going around that way with no idea of the dangers she was going into.

At Waterloo we had a very nice lunch of home-made bread and butter, coffee, and luscious strawberries, the first we have seen and only a half franc, ten cents, a plate. My whole trip, including lunch, cost eighty-five cents. I enclose a daisy which I picked up right on the battlefield.

The old Scotch guide when I told him I had seen the great battlefields of the United States wanted to know if I knew Grant and Sherman, and was delighted when I told him I had been the wife of a general.

Brussels—Last Thursday Mrs. Wood's friend, Mrs. Peyser, took us to ride in her beautiful victoria behind her handsome team with its gold-mounted harness. We have seen the Palais de Justice, the largest court building in the world, and also the antique part of the Museum of Fine Arts. I am no judge of art but I wish to say right here that I am a convert of the Dutch school. What I have seen here and in the great galleries of Rotterdam and Amsterdam have converted me. Oh! if you could just see the cattle pictures by Verboeckhoven. The sheep just stand and look at you, and in one picture is the great grand head of an ox with big horns. In Amsterdam we saw pictures of chickens, yes, chickens and roosters that crowed. In the Brussels Museum are two Rembrandts and a half dozen by Van Dyck, but I did not care for them and neither did I care for the pictures by Titian. Of course the fault is in me.

I have seen the Hotel de Ville with its graceful towers and its priceless Gobelin tapestries. The building is still used as the municipal building of Brussels, and in a room hung with priceless Gobelins the city council holds its meetings. Perhaps your mayor would like something of that kind.

Just back of the Hotel de Ville is the Mannikin Fountain, always called by the natives "Mannikin pis." The little fellow stands right at the corner and is just the size in bronze that he was in life when his noble father found the little runaway and the fountain comes out in a steady stream, very naturally as the child was doing when he was found. On fête days the statue is put in court dress and when it rains an umbrella is put over it. A queer fancy.

A kiss and love to each one.

Ellen S. Mussey.

Russell Square, London, W. C.
May 12, 1900.

My dear Folks at Home: Imagine me seated in my room before a real English open fire, pretending I am very warm and comfortable when in reality the chills are running down my back. The maid says it is a very nice fire and that the room is cheerful. The coal pot is not over six inches deep and fifteen inches across the front, and the pretty red-cheeked maid brought "the coals" and the kindling wood in a piece of newspaper. Nearly the middle of May, and I have on all my winter underwear and this morning I wore my heavy black jacket and yet was cold all the time.

I ordered a bottle of Scotch whisky before I went out and have just taken a good drink of it without spoiling it with water. I find the bottle charged on my bills at 3-6, which is eighty-six cents of our money. It is a quart bottle and excellent whisky. Mrs. Wood paid six francs—$1.20—for a half pint of whisky in Paris. That shows the difference in some things.

. . . We saw Queen Victoria when she came to London on Thursday morning. We were on the bus and the driver said, "'Ere comes the Old Lady." She was riding in an open carriage in the rain, a picture of serenity. We got a good view of her.

Yesterday was the first bright sunny warm day, and I improved it by going to Windsor with a Miss G———, also an American. We had an early breakfast and then walked down to take the bus for Paddington Station. We climbed up on top of the bus and immediately the driver, a jolly, red-faced Englishman, took an interest in us. He told us where Dickens lived and pointed out various places of interest on the way. We passed Marylebone Chapel, built by Sir Christopher Wren, in which are the famous Bow Bells, passed Madam Tussaud's show, and finally were set down at Paddington Station and got into our second-class compartment. It is plenty good enough for any decent person. Quite as good as our ordinary coaches and perfectly comfortable unless you have a long journey.

There is no grass like that in England. The constant drizzle keeps everything such a fresh beautiful green, and we enjoyed our ride so much. Presently we crossed the Thames and caught a glimpse of stately old Windsor Castle. We jumped into a hansom, said, "Castle," and were jolting up the hill but found it was a mere step instead of the half mile we had been told, but we paid our one shilling, six pence, all the same.

Then we walked on the terrace and saw the lovely views and prowled around the buildings and, finding nothing was open until twelve, made a bargain with a man to take us to Eton and Stoke Poges. Away we went in the lovely May morning with the sun shining and the birds singing. We crossed the Thames and began to meet the Eton boys with their tall silk hats and round jackets, the older ones with regular swallow-tailed coats on. The guide book says they "represent a large section of the wealth and aristocracy of England." We went through the quaint old chapel, which is of the time of Henry VI, and we thought of all the famous men who had been educated there.

Then we went on past picturesque English cottages, pretentious villas, and a few beautiful mansions until our driver stopped at a gate and we alighted at the dearest old cottage of all, old stone, overgrown with ivy, and nestled down in a great flower garden. A sweet-faced woman bade us go on to the church, which was open, and there before us was Stoke Poges, the scene pictured in Gray's "Elegy." The scene, the time, the weather were all perfect. I have a picture of the churchyard and the church to show you, but I cannot give you the coloring or the sound of the cuckoo that was calling, calling, all the time we were there.

Gray and his mother are buried in one grave. The epitaph is the poet's own. "The mother of seven children of whom one had the misfortune to survive her." Growing beside the grave is a yew tree three hundred years old.

We drove back to Windsor in time to see St. George's Chapel while it was still open. Then we were tired and hungry and went off to have lunch, a "hot-joint"—roast beef, potatoes, and beer, all good.

After that we were shown around the Royal Mews, in other words, the horse stables, by a very nice young groom. Of course we felt as though we were quite a part of royalty after seeing the grays that draw the Queen, the strawberry roans she has recently purchased, and the chestnuts which the visitors and the gentlemen and ladies of the 'ousehold use. There was the Queen's donkey also and the Shetland ponies for the royal children, and state carriages, and "brakes for baggage," and the Queen's new garden chair, and the old one which the donkey draws, etc., etc.—one hundred horses and eighty carriages, not to mention the gold-mounted harness galore.

We saw the riding room where the royal children are taught to ride and the horses are trained. In the gallery is the Queen's room where she sits and watches the proceedings if she is so minded.

It was here last week the Queen dined her returned middies and sent them 100 bottles of old port. Everyone loves the Queen.

Today I have been to the House of Parliament. It is only open to visitors on Saturday. It is very stately, very grand, and the chambers of the House of Lords and the House of Commons are very dark and small. There are only 450 seats in the Commons and 657 members so it is no unusual sight to see many members standing up.

My friends here are trying to get a card from a member to admit me to the strangers' gallery. They say if I were not a woman, I would at once, as a distinguished person, be sent a card, but a woman has to go behind a certain screened gallery. How odd! It seems I am a very remarkable woman over here, an L. L. M. and a member of the bar of the Supreme Court of the United States. Now please treat me with respect.

To me the most interesting part was Westminster Hall. Here Cromwell was proclaimed Lord Protector and a few years later his body was dragged from its resting place in the abbey, his head cut off, and stuck on a pinnacle of this same Westminster Hall, where it hung for over twenty-five years until one night the wind blew it down, and a sentry picked it up and sold it to a member of the Cromwell family.

I had a lovely time in Westminster Abbey. Stayed an hour and will go back another time. I only visited the statesmen and the poets' corner, but it was rich in sentiment and wonderful to see the tablets to the memory of Dickens, Tennyson, Dryden, "Rare" Ben Jonson, Disraeli, and others.

We also went to Westminster Bridge to get a fine view of the House of Parliament. Then I was chilled through, so after a lunch of hot chocolate, rolls, cold ham, and ginger cake, we took a bus to Peter Robinson's and shortly were pricing goods, etc. It is a very large and excellent department store. I went with a friend, not intending to buy, but I was tempted into purchasing a piece of black silk striped net for a waist for myself. Will I have money enough to get home? Some things are very cheap and some very high. For instance, cotton underwear is fully twice as high as at home. I have a fine new golf cape which at home would have cost $30 but here it was $18.50. It is black and red.

I have been to see the famous Tower of London, and to the Royal Academy which opened May 7, also through a part of the National Gallery. It is immense, but after walking through miles and miles of masterpieces one does not look at them with the same interest as when one started.

I have a catalogue for the Royal Academy. I blundered in there in rubbers and a rainy day get-up to find that it was a dress affair. However, I had paid my shilling and as no one knew me, I went on. (Mrs. W——— does not know, so don't mention it.)

Am so glad that in two weeks I shall be sailing toward the United States. Had a letter from Mr. T——— and he made my mouth water by telling me of dear Betty's Sunday evening supper, chicken, salad, biscuit, and strawberries. We live well here but it is not Betty's.

Love to all of you and regards to friends,

Ellen S. Mussey.

London, May 18, 1900.

Dear Folks at Home: Well, Sunday I was fifty years old and celebrated by going to service in Westminster Abbey. Think of that! It was a special service with a sermon by the archbishop to the Thirteenth Volunteer Company of Middlesex about to sail for the Transvaal. It was fine and impressive and very English. The congregation joined in singing "We are Volunteers in the Army of the Lord," and it sounded and reverberated through those wonderful vaulted aisles in a way never to be forgotten. A——— was waiting for me at the door, and after seeing the regiment march away, we went around to Parliament House to see the old woman feed the doves.

I spent a day in St. Paul's and Westminster by myself and enjoyed very much rambling through Paternoster Row, Ludgate Hill, etc., all places I had longed to see. Yesterday I visited schools and afterward went on top of an omnibus through the real poverty-stricken district of Whitechapel. . . .

This afternoon I am to speak at a meeting of the New Church Women's League. It seems they have never before been addressed by a woman. Next Monday I go to Oxford for two days and then I take a day to ride by coach through Warwick, Stratford-on-Avon, and Kenilworth. Well, it will soon be over and I will be on the briny deep.

With love and kisses to each of you,

Ellen S. Mussey.

Mrs. Mussey visited the law college at Oxford and was the guest at a luncheon given by one of the students. She was informed by a don that three women were studying law at the college and that they had completed the prescribed course but, because they were women, they would not receive degrees.

While Mrs. Mussey was at Oxford, a ceremony was held at which members of an Australian delegation were given honorary degrees, and arrangements were made for her to attend this event. But being a woman, she was not allowed to sit with the dons but was given a place next to them, on a lower level.

Chapter XV

OPINIONS

To Mrs. Mussey's surprise the law college continued to function. Each year the number of students increased and each year more members of the bar gave their services as instructors. Without pay, too, and without hope of any, Mrs. Mussey was sure, because there was not the slightest indication that this school would ever pay its own way. The more students there were, the greater the cost of up-keep. Ends seemed never to meet.

Yet someone had to provide a place for women to study law and Dean Mussey and Miss Gillett could do nothing but go on with their financial struggle. And go on with the fight against eternal skepticism, too, for it was always breaking out unexpectedly.

At commencements and banquets speakers who had readily accepted invitations from this school established for women were as like as not to take advantage of the occasion to air their prejudices against women, and to warn the young ladies of the "conditions of their sex."

But upon rare occasions there came a treasured and soul-satisfying speaker who fairly emanated inspiration by his whole-hearted approval and encouragement. Such a one was Wu Ting-fang, Minister from China, the guest of honor at the college banquet in 1902. Dressed in the full regalia of his Chinese costume, flowing robes of silk and ermine, a man from a country where it was generally supposed women were considered inferior, yet so enthusiastic was Minister Wu about the cause of woman that he talked until one o'clock in the morning.

"When I studied law," he said, "I had no idea that ladies would study law, too. But my eyes are open now and I see no valid reason why the legal profession should not be open to women as well as men.

"What more evidence do you want?" he asked, "than the eloquence and intellect of this affair tonight to demonstrate the superiority of the American woman? I wish I possessed part of the intellect possessed by the women gathered here. Are they not good talkers? And is it not almost impossible for a man to convince a woman while it is easy for a woman to convince a man?"

He also advocated jury service for women. "To avoid a miscarriage of justice, if the offender is a woman, the jury should be composed of women," he declared. "Why? Because their minds could not be abused by sympathy. It is also a worthy object of consideration that women should not sit on a jury when the prisoner is a man? Why? There is too much leaning to the opposite sex in this world. A man should be tried by his peers—men; a woman by her peers—women."

But in the very wake of Minister Wu's fervency came an irksome dose of conservatism. The commencement speaker, Jonathan P. Dolliver, United States Senator of Iowa, told the graduates that they should get married instead of practicing law.

"I must confess I have old-fashioned ideas," admitted Senator Dolliver, "and while I believe the women can plead a case as well as anyone else, my advice to them is to get married and settle down—the best any of you can do is to settle down with a man."

It was apparently quite beyond the senator that a woman might marry and still be a lawyer. Yet many married women were practicing law, and at this very time, serving on the Board of Trustees of the College and also on the teaching staff was a married couple, Elijah C. Foster and J. Ellen Foster, and both of them were lawyers. Furthermore, Mrs. Foster was the mother of two children.

Another skeptical gentleman was Leslie M. Shaw, Secretary of the Treasury, who was the guest of honor at the banquet of 1903. Mr. Shaw took it upon himself to warn the young women not to try to become jury lawyers. He asserted that women were not adapted to that sort of practice and cautioned them not to attempt the impossible but to select those branches of practice for which they were best fitted by nature.

Mrs. Mussey could not let this go unchallenged and she told Mr. Shaw that he needed coaching as to the possibilities that awaited women in the law. "Women are adaptable to any branch of practice," she assured him.

When J. Holdsworth Gordon, President of the District Bar Association, addressed the graduating class of 1904 he expressed a belief in the equality of the sexes. "Some men," he averred, "have the audacity to insist that women are never first in anything except sin, but I look over the world and see women at the forefront in the realm of commerce, the professions, in science, and almost every branch of industry. I say throw down the bars and let them in, and let it be the survival of the fittest."

That, of course, was all that these women studying law could reasonably ask for and most of them had come to Washington as government workers in search of this very opportunity. But they had found that even the government placed limitations upon them, simply because they were women. For many positions, particularly in the higher salaried classes, were closed to women. An example of the attitude toward women's salaries, that had been extreme in its application, had occurred in Grover Cleveland's second administration.

John G. Carlysle, of Kentucky, appointed Secretary of the Treasury by Mr. Cleveland, thought that no women should receive high salaries, and when he found that several women of the Treasury Department were receiving as much as $1600 a year, he set about at once to investigate and reduce their pay. One case was that of Miss Mary Brady, a woman who had refused all political influence to gain favor and had risen entirely upon her merits.

It proved difficult to find fault with Miss Brady's record, but the Secretary was a determined man and the story was told that when he discovered in the course of his investigation that Miss Brady in all the years she had been working for the government, had never taken a day of sick leave, he concluded with vehemence that such a woman must be a "damned curiosity" and thereupon reduced her pay to $1400. But such unfair views could not endure, the next administration made amends, and women slowly worked their way into better-paid positions.

The law school founded by Mrs. Mussey and Miss Gillett paved the way for this advancement because a knowledge of the law was of invaluable aid in many branches of government service. And women, ambitious to get ahead, worked at their jobs through the day and attended law school at night.

Other women, too, were interested in studying law and they came to Washington, not only from all parts of the United States, but from foreign countries. From Uruguay came Pepita Larroque, the daughter of a large family, selected to study law because she seemed the one best fitted to manage the family fortune. From Sweden came Lydia Hendrickson, who was chancellor of the Swedish legation and felt the need of a knowledge of the law in her work.

There were women, too, of all ages, young girls still in their teens, middle-aged women who had raised families. In the second graduating class was Miss Helen R. Hill, of Laurel, Maryland, who was not yet twenty-one, and Mrs. Jennie Munroe, of Virginia, a grandmother. Mrs. Munroe was the first woman appointed to the contest division of the General Land Office, and for a long time the only woman in that division.

But while some women were forging ahead, others were still expending their energies in the struggle against tradition and the ingrained prejudices regarding women's place in the scheme of things. For there were communities where women of the law were unheard of, where they would be looked upon as queer, or bold, or not quite nice.

This was the condition faced by Miss Sarah Grogan, of Elberton, Georgia. In her circle it was not considered proper for a woman to go outside the home to earn her living at any occupation. And for a woman to be a lawyer was so unthinkable that Miss Grogan, imbued with a desire to study law, dared not even whisper that she harbored such an ambition.

For she had already sorely wounded the family pride, perhaps even the community pride, by going into government service in Washington, D. C. Her father was particularly distressed and he told her feelingly that it was with shame and mortification he informed anyone that his daughter was in Washington, working for the government.

If she were to take a still more radical step and study law, Miss Grogan feared she would be ostracized by her family and friends. But her desire for a legal education was so intense that at last she conceived a plan whereby she might follow her inclinations and still save the family pride. In 1901, she went to the school founded by Mrs. Mussey and Miss Gillett and enrolled as a student under an assumed name, Virginia Washington Post, Virginia for the state in which she had gone to school and Washington Post for a Washington newspaper that she greatly admired.

She told Dean Mussey her real name, however, and explained the situation that made a pseudonym necessary. The secret was safe with the dean, and throughout the three-year law course Miss Grogan's friends and associates never guessed her dual rôle. When she was invited out for the evening, she pleaded a previous engagement and went to her law classes. When friends expressed surprise at her extreme popularity she merely smiled and said nothing. But at the end of the three-year law course, Miss Grogan began to feel a new courage in her venture and she was graduated in her own name.

But she could not be a lawyer in her home state. Georgia did not admit women to the bar. Other states, too, still denied women the right to practice law. Among them were Arkansas, Delaware, Tennessee, and Virginia. But Maryland had at last capitulated to the advancement of women. Two and a half centuries after Mistress Brent's able legal services in behalf of the colony, Maryland passed a law, giving women the right of admission to the bar.

CHAPTER XVI

WORK AND PLAY

The District of Columbia, in 1902, was given a new law regarding justices of the peace, and it occurred to Attorney W. J. Newton, who was a champion of women in the law, that one of these posts should be given to a woman and that Miss Emma Gillett, with whom he had formed a law partnership, was unusually well qualified for such a place. Mr. Newton asked Mrs. Mussey to discuss the matter with the President, Theodore Roosevelt, who had recently taken office following the death of William McKinley.

Mrs. Mussey wished to make a favorable impression upon Mr. Roosevelt, and aware that even a President might harbor distorted views of women who practiced law, she prepared for this contingency. She took with her to the White House Mrs. Nanette B. Paul and Miss Gertrude Leonard, young ladies of the law school who were not only alert exponents of the legal profession but unusually attractive young women as well.

The President was very cordial. He told Mrs. Mussey that he had known General Mussey and spoke of him in the most complimentary terms. Then, with a keen look at Mrs. Mussey and one of his great hearty laughs, Mr. Roosevelt remarked, "Somehow, you don't look like I thought the woman dean of a law school should look."

When Mrs. Mussey asked him about his policy concerning women in public office, he assured her that whenever the appointment of women was permitted under the law, he would consider them on their merits. But he was in doubt about the law regarding justices of the peace and he told Mrs. Mussey to call upon the Attorney General, Philander C. Knox, to find out if women might be appointed.

To facilitate her interview with Mr. Knox, the President gave Mrs. Mussey his card. It was black-bordered because of the death of Mr. McKinley, and Mr. Roosevelt seemed very much distressed that none but mourning cards were available. He directed an aide at once to order plain cards.

The meeting with Mr. Knox was somewhat gratifying but futile. "Why didn't you come sooner?" he exclaimed. "Of course we could appoint women, but men have been named for all the places now and everything is settled except the final approval of the President." Mr. Knox said he had encountered a great deal of difficulty in finding suitable candidates and that he would have been glad to consider a woman qualified for the job.

In October, 1902, the Grand Army of the Republic held its national encampment in Washington, and Mrs. Mussey was appointed chairman of the committee in charge of entertainment of the women's auxiliary organizations. It was the sort of job Mrs. Mussey loved because it meant numerous festivities, meeting interesting and well-known people. Zestfully she made plans to give the visitors something outstanding in the way of Washington hospitality. Confident that nothing could please them more than an opportunity to greet the nation's First Lady, Mrs. Mussey wrote to Mrs. Roosevelt and asked her to receive the women of the G. A. R.

But it was not so easy to go to the White House now. The Roosevelts had put a stop to public receptions; they had limited other receptions; they had even locked the gates to the rear grounds of the White House. The Executive Mansion was becoming somewhat exclusive. Mrs. Roosevelt, however, consented to receive the women of the G. A. R., upon two conditions. The number of guests must be limited to one thousand and a suitable place must be provided for the reception.

The White House at this time was undergoing extensive alterations, the Roosevelts were living on Jackson Place, opposite Lafayette Square, and this house was too small for so large a gathering. Mrs. Mussey sought a reception room at various hotels but the prices were exorbitant. One hotel asked $500 for an afternoon reception, which was quite beyond the committee's means.

Finally, Mrs. Mussey asked for the use of the Corcoran Art Gallery. Requests had been made for this building for other encampment meetings and they had been refused, but a reception to be given by Mrs. Roosevelt—that was different. The Corcoran opened its doors in welcome. Limiting the number of guests to one thousand, however, was a poser. For there were twelve hundred women delegates and all of them would want to attend the reception. It was too delicate a task for Mrs. Mussey and her committee, and they left it to the discretion of the auxiliary organizations.

The latter decided that above all others the nurses of the Civil War deserved invitations and they were supplied first. Then other delegates, according to rank and service, were given cards. But two hundred women had to be left out and they were bitterly disappointed. Tears flowed profusely, for this was the most desirable social event of the whole encampment.

Others in Washington were also gnashing their teeth over this reception. No sooner did the news get out that Mrs. Roosevelt was to receive, than hosts of people in no way connected with the G. A. R. came clamoring for invitations. Washingtonians had become accustomed to being received by the mistress of the White House and they regarded it as their right. One senator even came to Mrs. Mussey's office and demanded a certain number of invitations. But they were not forthcoming.

The fortunate one thousand who were invited literally beamed with happiness, particularly the nurses, and they asked as a special favor that they be allowed to keep their cards instead of relinquishing them at the door, so that they might have a memento of Mrs. Roosevelt's hospitality. Mrs. Mussey and the committee members were pleased beyond measure by this feeling on the part of the nurses. Of course they might keep their cards.

And the nurses were among the first guests to arrive at the reception. Mrs. Mussey introduced them to Mrs. Roosevelt, who was assisted by the ladies of the cabinet. Soon the Corcoran Gallery was thronged with gay and happy women. It was a most charming party, and Mrs. Mussey could not help feeling regret that two hundred women had had to be denied this pleasure.

But by and by, word was brought to her that a count had been kept of the number of guests as they arrived, that a thousand women had already been admitted, but others were still coming, and all of them had cards. Yet only a thousand invitations had been issued. An investigation was made at once.

The committee found that it had been tricked. The compassionate nurses, well trained in the alleviation of suffering, had hit upon the plan of passing their cards, supposed to be kept as souvenirs, to the unfortunate delegates who had not been invited. But the ruse was discovered before all the extra women could be admitted.

The chief topic of conversation at the reception was the President's health. He had received a severe leg injury in a collision while traveling in New England, and the ladies were solicitous about him. Mrs. Roosevelt said he suffered a great deal of pain but that he was the most patient man in the world.

This was the praise of a devoted and indulgent wife, Mrs. Mussey thought, for only that morning when she passed the temporary White House she had seen Mr. Roosevelt frothing and swearing in a paroxysm of anger that bespoke anything but patience when attendants, assisting him from his carriage, hurt his injured leg. He had continued to rage all the way into the house, and later Mrs. Mussey was told by an attendant that the President had become so wrought up it had been necessary to call Mrs. Roosevelt to quiet him.

Mrs. Mussey's law practice had increased rapidly, and in the spring of 1905, weary from multitudinous duties, she decided upon a trip to Europe, going alone this time, because that seemed a more restful way to travel. She wrote often to her family.

June 16, 1905.

Dear Ones: Last night was foggy and the fog horn blew frequently during the night. My roommate is a Miss C——— from Philadelphia and she is so afraid of the water. She stood it until three this morning when she had to have human sympathy. She is going with her father to Gibraltar.

I find a great many acquaintances on board, at least twenty-five, some from Washington and some from other places. My next neighbor at table is a young lawyer of Alexandria and he's good company. Mrs. H———, the milliner, is on board and has two friends with her.

The sea is as smooth as glass today, and this vessel is an easy goer but it is very crowded. The food is just passable. I am at the first table, for which I am thankful. The second breakfast does not begin until nine A. M. which would be quite too late for me.

Saturday, June 17—The third day out and fine weather. No fog and no fog horn last night so we all slept well. I rather think that after I leave Rome I may travel to Cologne with Mrs. H——— and her two friends. They want to travel about as I do and four is a good number for carriage hire.

There are about 400 Italians in the steerage. They pay $18 to go back home and have their three meals a day including wine. We go often to look down on them.

I wish you could all have some of this cool salt air. I have never seen such deep blue water as we are churning through now.

Sunday, June 18—We saw, early this morning, our first vessel but it was soon lost to view. There was divine service this morning in the second cabin, but I did not go down. The air is cool but heavy and I felt so sleepy.

We had our first excitement this morning, a fire in the steerage. It destroyed some bedding and clothing of a poor Italian and there was quite a tumult. The Anglo-Saxons worked to put out the fire and the Italians got down on their knees and prayed to God and the Virgin to put it out.

We made 317 miles yesterday and are not half way to the Azores. It is not yet sure that we can land there.

I had my first talk with the captain today. He is an Englishman about 35 or 40. He knew about me and said he had directed that I sit at his table. Our table steward is a fine one. He is very young and he hustles for our food in fine fashion. For Betty's information I will say that at lunch today I had grilled spring chicken, French fried potatoes, salad, cottage pudding, cheese and crackers and black coffee. The cheese was an Italian cheese rather like Roquefort.

Monday, June 19—Our first rough sea! The rolling began about noon and we have had head winds and white caps ever since and now there is a driving rain. I am glad to say that I suffer no inconvenience so far from the heavy seas, but there are quite a number who do.

Tuesday, June 20—It is so cold that I can't stay outside and am too lazy to go down and put on my winter underwear. I am wearing a knit underskirt, my heavy winter walking skirt, a silk waist, my heavy woolen sweater, and golf cape.

Wednesday, June 21—This is our finest day, sea and air and sky all perfect. Last night I did not sleep well because my little room-mate was sick. It is now a week since we left terra firma behind us but we expect to see land tonight.

June 22—We hope to stop at Ponta Delgada on the Azores about three this afternoon. I had a long talk last night with the captain and he says the Portuguese gardens at the islands are well worth seeing. The captain is the most interesting man I have conversed with so far.

I find my long-sleeved flannel undervest very comfortable indeed and am wearing also a flannel corset cover and heavy rainy-day skirt with knit underskirt. What more would I wear in midwinter? It is the penetrating sea air, I suppose. As mails are so uncertain at the Azores, I'll not send this letter until we reach Gibraltar.

Your devoted

E. S. Mussey.

June 23—We landed yesterday at Ponta Delgada. Along the ridge are well-tilled fields of corn and tobacco, etc., divided by low green hedges. We saw no fences. We saw several Portuguese villages, quaint houses colored white, pink, blue, and yellow.

When we anchored, small rowboats came out to carry us to shore. They were manned by wild, barefooted creatures who proved to be good oarsmen. We went down the high ship's side on swinging ladders and had to make a flying leap of about four feet to the open boat. I knocked the man flat who was to receive my fairy form and we both sat down very hard in the bottom of the boat, looking, as some one said, like a pair of wrestlers. Unfortunately, I hurt my foot so today I cannot promenade the deck as usual.

A party of five of us took a carriage for two hours at an expense to each of sixty cents and we drove around the quaint streets, saw the Spanish señoritas on their balconies, leaning over the half doors as we see in the old pictures. They still have the latticed and barred windows of Spanish countries. It was the festival of St. Christopher, and there were many processions. The people were all in gala dress but to our regret all the shops were closed.

The tropical gardens were perfectly wonderful, such fuchsias climbing over the high walls, such great ferns growing in extinct volcanoes, great trees covered with spiky crimson blossoms, borders of immense poppies, and everywhere, banana trees, orange trees, and palm-bordered walks. We came away laden with lilies, crimson hibiscus, and immense marguerites.

We went into one quaint cathedral about 400 years old and oh! the beggars. They were as plentiful as the flowers and so terribly swollen with disease. We got back to the ship for dinner and sat on deck until midnight watching the fireworks on shore.

June 25, nearing Gibraltar—I am going to write baby ——— a postal from every place I visit and I want them kept for her until she is old enough to be interested in them. I do hope you are all well. I begin to feel a little more alive, not so dead and numb.

June 26—We sailed into the straits of Gibraltar early this morning and the ship was alive. By eight o'clock we were going off in the tender to the shore.

Our party of five took a carriage with a driver who spoke English and we drove around to the wonderful English fort and the beautiful gardens on the side of the rock and through the narrow oriental streets where Arabs, Turks, Spaniards, and English hob-nob, and then we drove around the great rock, across the neutral ground, beyond the Victoria Garden to Spain.

After leaving the customs house we passed into the worst town of all Spain, all dust and squalor. I got a few things as souvenirs, including several Spanish bull fight fans and a dear little brass brazier which I always wanted.

The great rock is pierced with portholes and is even bigger than it seems and the way the poor horses and little carts run up the sides is frightful.

June 30, 1905.

My dear Ones: Early yesterday morning we anchored in the much lauded Bay of Naples, but there we were kept while we were thoroughly fumigated and every one of the 400 steerage passengers vaccinated. We saw the yellow flag run up at our masthead and learned for the first time that there was a case of smallpox in the steerage. It was a hot and weary experience and I do not love the Bay of Naples.

However, we landed at last, ran the gauntlet of the customs house and the riff-raff of Naples, and drove to "Parkers" upon the heights. It was daintily clean with tiled floors, much marble, and many frescoes. We drove for three hours up, up the hill, past lovely gardens and villas and, as it was a fête day—St. Peter's—we saw many shrines by the roadside and in the private grounds, beautifully decorated and lighted.

Then we came down into the old town and saw the big cows and little calves going around to attend to customers. The cow was milked into a glass jar at every customer's door. The poorer people were served by goats which go through the streets in droves. They are also fed in the streets.

July 2—Have just taken a look at old Vesuvius. She is spouting fire at a great rate. It was an interesting spectacle. I hear the herds of goats passing as I write and the herders have a peculiar cry.

Since Thursday night we have visited the ruins of Pompeii and they surpass my wildest imaginings but oh! what a hot day was that. After resting for the night, we went to Paestum to see those wonderful temples, built five hundred years before Christ and standing now in imposing grandeur as a monument to the civilization of that age and an enigma to the scholars of today.

At Salerno we found open carriages awaiting us as by arrangement and began our drive around the Gulf of Salerno to Sorrento, twenty-five miles of perfect road, made and kept in order by the Italian government. Such views! such vineyards! such groves of lemons, almonds, apricots! We rested for the night at a quaint old place at Amalfi and went to sleep to the music of the lapping waves.

At Sorrento we put up at a pension which was formerly a monastery. It is right on the Bay of Naples and is said to be a thousand years old. We have delicious fruits, apricots, plums, peaches, pears, cherries, and fine vegetables. These Italian hotels are so far daintily neat, all tiled floors and white marble and I like the food except the bread and butter and there is no ice.

Mrs. H——— does all the bargaining for us and she does it well. Last night our bill for dinner, room, and breakfast this morning was $1.20 each and I had a separate room.

Rome, July 8—The best thing that happened to me in Rome was the receipt of my first letter from home. I am so glad E——— concluded to cut some more teeth early in the season and that she did not get sick during that very hot weather.

D——— writes that business is dull and safe.

I arrived here last Monday, the hottest day Rome had seen in over thirty years and such a time as they made about it. It was no worse than it often is in Washington and the nights here are always more comfortable. But in deference to the warnings of the natives I try to stay indoors from 1 to 3.30 P. M. I thought to do Rome pretty well in ten days but it would take ten months. This is the treasure house of the ages.

Mrs. H———, her two friends, and I have a carriage together for three days for $3.00 a day and a tip of forty cents. The driver speaks English very well, is a good guide as well as driver, and saves us a good deal by managing that we go to certain museums and galleries on the free, instead of the pay days. But these places resemble, in some ways, a circus as to side shows and extra fees. . . .

The first night I was here I rode down in the "tram" to see St. Peter's, and half hidden behind it, the Vatican, with the two Swiss guards at the corridor to prevent intrusion on His Holiness. We crossed the Tiber on the tram and came to the great plaza with the immense obelisk and fountain in the foreground. Around the fountain are always gathered the poor, especially the children and beggars. The great dome of St. Peter's is more imposing than you would imagine from the pictures.

Yesterday two Catholic friends took us to the Sacristry in St. Peter's to see the vestments and jewels of the Pope. It was gorgeous. For an extra franc we were allowed to see the chariots of the different Popes. They are much handsomer than those at Windsor Castle. We saw today the original "Aurora," and I mean to treat myself to an engraving of it if I can get a good one at a decent price.

. . . You remember that the poets write of the groves of Vallombrosa, three thousand feet above Florence. I am going there for a day or so and I want a little glimpse of the Apennines. Doesn't the name sound good?

Have got my laundry done, my skirt and blouses cleaned, hair washed, watch mended, and am ready to travel until Aug. 12, just five weeks from today, when I sail for home.

Florence, July 14—I had an audience with the Pope on Sunday afternoon in company with about 150 other persons, two-thirds of whom were Americans, the others, pilgrims of the continent, some of them suffering from afflictions. We had been instructed how to dress. A woman must not wear a hat but have her head covered with a lace scarf and be dressed in black. Lots of the party had trouble getting the proper head covering.

At the foot of the broad stairway leading to the reception room we were told to remove gloves and we went slowly up the stairs under careful watch.

The Pope was dressed in white and looked most benign. He gave his message in Italian, which was translated by his secretary, "In so far as a Pope may, I bless you all."

Then he passed about the room blessing each individual and everyone kissed his ring.

. . . We took the lovely ride over the Appian Way, past many tombs, to the catacombs which we visited with a very jolly priest for a guide. We passed the baths of Caracalla which accommodated 10,000 persons and were free. We passed the great circus of Romulus where 15,000 could witness the great chariot races. It makes "Ben Hur" and "Quo Vadis" seem real. There are enough circuses in and around Rome to please even D———.

One morning I spent on the Palatine Hill visiting the ruined homes of the Caesars. A sightly spot it is, looking over the Eternal

City to the Vatican and down into the ruined Forum. The Emperors builded their palaces on top of those of their predecessors so that their glories should not survive. The ancients seem to have had the same jealousies as those of the present day.

July 15—Florence is hot but delightful. The Apennines are all around and lovely against the Italian blue sky. The river is a peculiar green. The bridges are numerous and picturesque and one of them is covered with shops.

We have been to the galleries and have seen all kinds of Madonnas and babies and Christs and disciples. We have visited the principal churches and the great cathedral. The latter looks best in pictures. The interior is bare and disappointing.

. . . I guess my new brown silk will be rags and tatters by the time I get out of Italy, but I can't endure woolen skirts in this climate. We are glad to say that the fleas are not so bad here but we are promised their society in Venice with mosquitoes added. There is to be a national fête in Venice on Monday, so we may hope to see the Grand Canal illuminated. But I dread the journey from 2.30 to 9.40 from Florence to Venice. They do not hurry here and they call the locomotive the "machine."

On Lake Como, July 21—Here I am on this lovely lake almost within hailing distance of the Alps. I have a corner room with two windows right on the lake and it is a picture never to be forgotten.

. . . Venice is gorgeous, dirty and fascinating. The Grand Canal, with its graceful gondolas and gondoliers, was most interesting. I like gondolas better than cabs. In front of our hotel, facing the Grand Canal, were always at least a dozen gondolas waiting to be called, just like cabs in other cities.

In Venice every peasant woman, young or old, has a long black shawl in which she wraps herself. It must cover a multitude of sins and dirt. And the well-to-do peasants, men and women, abound in jewelry, especially earrings.

The Italians are very human and so tender with their bambinos. A child seems to call forth the greatest tenderness from everyone. I also saw a dozen people halt to rescue a wee kitten that had fallen into the Grand Canal. A boy climbed down and got it and a gondolier left his business to assist in the good work and everybody else gave advice and rejoiced when the poor creature was saved.

The male Italian is amusing. His fierce mustaches and his amorous eyes conflict. The young girls are very attractive, but the older women rarely are.

I would at this minute pay two dollars if I could take Sunday evening supper with Betty and have some of her coffee and bread and butter. Italian cooking is usually good, but good bread and coffee are unknown.

July 23, Lugano, Switzerland—We came over here yesterday to order our circular or "Abandon" tickets, as they are called, for fifteen days of unlimited travel in Switzerland. We have to have our photos taken to put on the ticket and then we can roam at will for the sum of ten dollars.

This morning while the rest of the party went to church, I took a steamer trip of 52 miles, fare thirty cents in our money. We kept crossing and recrossing the border line of Italy and Switzerland and the customs inspectors were kept busy looking at the baggage and putting on their funny little labels.

One place on this lake is particularly beautiful—a ruined castle, an old church on the point, and a charming arcade and row of high trimmed trees along the lake front. By the way, I met in Venice Miss L——— who is conducting a party of nine. It is a nice way to make money. One lady who has a party will clear $2,000 and have her own trip free.

. . . This is a good hotel right on the lake and I have a front room at $1.20 a day, meals included. At Lucerne we hear there is a great crowd and prices are way up.

I shall be very happy to be home again just one month from today but I dread the heat. Get ready the ice-cold water melons, the juicy peaches, and the cantaloups. I have not seen a melon here, and the peaches are not like ours. I would like you to taste an omelette soufflé as it is produced at this hotel. It is a dream.

The hotel manager is a very, very tall "Italian" by the name of "Michael Maloney." How does that strike you for Italian?

Usually I feel pretty well but sometimes I am very weary.

July 30, Chamonix, France—Here I am in sight of the great glaciers, very comfortable in my thin black silk dress. It is a miracle. The smaller glacier of Mt. Blanc seems very near as if it were not more than a hundred yards away.

We rode all day through such scenery as beggars description. We had some very steep climbs and descents, but the horses were sure-footed and the driver careful. . . . We did not go further up the Jungfrau than Sheidigg. The Frau is not to be relied upon and on this day was enveloped in clouds half way up. These railroads are fine and we went third class in comfort.

I feel much better since my arrival in Switzerland, but it is not really cool even here. Last Friday I walked quite a distance to see the upper glacier and the perspiration rolled down my face while I looked at it.

Zurich, Aug. 4, 1905—This is my last letter before I sail to my dear United States, and I packed my trunk today and sent it direct to the steamer. From now on I shall travel with hand baggage only. We have just come in from a long carriage ride and I am writing while the others dress for dinner. The laces and embroideries are temptingly cheap but my purse is running low so I must not yield.

Geneva is a nice clean city and is the warmest place in this comfortable little country. We came here by fast express and did not stop at Bern as we intended because we were so glad to have ourselves and our baggage comfortably settled in a clean car with "toilette" convenience. It is not always that we enjoy such comfort.

In Geneva I got myself a very handsome gloria rain-proof dust-coat. It was made to order and fits. It cost about one-fourth what it would in Washington. Our pension in Geneva was wretched. I was hungry all the time.

Prepare yourselves to see a woman with a complexion like an Indian's but I have less nerves than when I started.

Aboard the T. S. S. Ryndam, Aug. 12, 1905—We set sail on a fine day and I like this vessel very much. Will mail this at Boulogne, where we stop this evening. I hope it will go by rapid mail via England and reach you before we land.

During the past week we traveled through the Black Forest to Baden Baden. It is an unique region. Later we went on to quaint old Heidelberg, where we saw the Auld Schloss, the University, and the Auld Bridge. . . .

We took a boat up the Rhine to Cologne. I am sorry to say that I was disappointed in the Rhine. I like our own Hudson River best.

It is so cool and lovely on the water, it is hard to realize how hot it is in New York and Washington, but heat or no heat I am happy to be going home to you all. We are due to land Aug. 22 at Hoboken but I must go right on to Washington and work.

Ellen S. Mussey.

Busy though she was with her own law school, Mrs. Mussey accepted still more educational tasks. In 1906 she was appointed a member of the Board of Education. That meant numerous Congressional hearings and endless struggles for school appropriations. For the District of Columbia schools were at the mercy of Congress, and all too often congressmen, bent on making a showing of economy, slashed the school budget.

Congressional economy was particularly evident in the purchase of school grounds. Land was sometimes bought with no provision for adequate schoolyards and the children had no place to play except a few crowded nooks and in the streets. As the population increased and traffic became more congested, this became a formidable problem. The one solution was the purchase of more land adjacent to the schools.

Mrs. Mussey went to a meeting of congressmen to urge an appropriation for this purpose. But the expenditure did not meet with general approval. One congressman from Brooklyn, N. Y., vehemently opposed buying land for playgrounds. "Let the kids play in the streets," he cried. "My kids play in the streets."

In time, however, he relented somewhat and little by little money for larger schoolgrounds was appropriated. Congressmen sometimes wanted to try out their pet theories on the District of Columbia. One western senator declared that it was a bad thing for teachers to be too sure of their jobs, and he advocated having them take annual examinations. But other congressmen felt that if a teacher had to prepare herself for examinations so often, she was apt to neglect the actual job of teaching and the western senator's theory was not put into practice.

Mrs. Mussey was a leader in the organization of atypical schools—special class rooms for children with mental and physical defects—and she also worked to establish truant schools for children who had not been in regular attendance. Congressmen, in general, favored this work and willingly voted the necessary funds.

As a member of the school board, Mrs. Mussey felt it her duty to keep in close touch with all phases of school work and school needs and she visited both white and colored schools. She thoroughly believed that there should be no color line in the matter of public service.

CHAPTER XVII

IN SCANDINAVIA

Mrs. Mussey went on another journey to Europe in 1909, this time to Norway and Sweden to see the two countries whose counselor she had been for so many years. On this tour she was accompanied by Miss Wilhelmina Hartmann, a Washington school teacher.

Attachés of the Norwegian Legation outlined the trip, supplied letters of introduction, and advised Mrs. Mussey to provide herself with cards stating that she was a barrister, Dean of the Washington College of Law, a member of the bar of the United States Supreme Court, and a member of the Board of Education; that such cards would admit her to many places that might otherwise be closed.

As usual Mrs. Mussey wrote numerous letters to her family.

June 25, 1909.

My dear ones at home: It is now by ship's time, 9:30, and I have had bath and breakfast, taken a few turns on deck, and got my steamer chair established out of the way of the drifting fog.

I sit on the captain's left at table and am the special care of the captain's own man. On the captain's right is a Mr. C——— who has been knighted by the King of Denmark. The Scandinavian fare is delightful so far. We have a variety of nice relishes and every known kind of cracker and bread.

The various attendants all seem to be prejudiced against fresh air and water. We have two wash stands in our stateroom, but our stewardess is loath to give us water for both.

June 26—Not a breath of air, and yet we see whitecaps as far as the eye can reach. I put on my low-necked gauze underwear this morning and feel my gray waist all too warm. Last night I found my cambric nightgown all I could endure for covering. The foghorn blew until five this morning.

There are 110 first class passengers, 100 second class, and 400 third class or steerage. These last are very well cared for and are nice looking people. The band plays for them on the lower deck every afternoon, and they dance with spirit.

We hear at evening the peculiar noise which means the wireless is at work. Six telegrams were posted yesterday. It would cost me only a dollar to send ten words to New York, but there is no hurry and nothing to say.

June 27—Sunday. A wretched, rainy day, and we are all huddled on one small part of the deck out of the rain. We are off the banks of Newfoundland but quite a way south of them. Yesterday we saw porpoises at play. They danced quite out of the water.

We are all delighted with the food. It is substantial yet dainty and so different from anything at home. The menu is in Norse and translated into English. A regular article is eels, sometimes dried and sometimes fresh and fried, but so far we Americans will not touch them. On this line they make all the desserts, including ice cream, fresh daily. On most of the lines the desserts are purchased in New York, enough to last the voyage out and back.

No clergyman has asked to hold services so we shall have none today, the captain says.

After a fine dinner, coffee was served in the smoking room and we sat and chatted until nearly ten o'clock when a great platter of many kinds of sandwiches was passed around. I ate one, but many ordered beer and ate and drank for an hour. So far I have seen only one lady smoke cigarettes. She is from California. As I write I hear overhead the constant tramp, tramp of the passengers taking their constitutionals. Eleven rounds make a mile. So far I have made three.

June 29—We are past the region of the icebergs and did not see any. The temperature in our stateroom is down to 51 and the heavy red blankets are very comfortable.

June 30—Our worst day, cold, rainy, and windy. I have on my long-sleeved high-necked, second weight underwear; flannel skirt; heavy stockings; and winter suit.

We are more than half way across. I continue to sleep well and eat a great deal. We live out of doors during the day and play cards in the smoking room in the evening. At ten P. M. they serve our seventh meal. I cut out four of them and stick to the regulation three a day.

July 1—We had a big discussion at breakfast on woman's rights. The captain agrees with me, but the other women at the table do not.

July 2—We shall see land tonight. They published a newspaper on board today.

July 3—Last night a little after ten we could see lights on islands off the coast of Scotland. I have learned to chew gum and like it.

July 4—Our last on board ship. We were to have service on deck but the weather is too bad. Last night the captain's supper was a great success. The dining room was draped in flags and we had speeches.

Leaving Christiansand, Norway, July 4, 1909—We made our landing at Christiansand in a fine mist. It is a picturesque harbor but has no pier and the passengers went off in a large tender. There will be some new American fashions in old town tonight. Every passenger proudly carried his American flag. They will visit Norway but they mean to return to the United States. Among the first-class passengers who left us here was a successful dentist from Brooklyn. He was returning to see his mother after thirteen years and I thought how hard it would be if I couldn't see my boy for thirteen years.

I saw a few flakes of snow today. The steam heat is on all over the ship and I have on my winter flannels.

Christiania, Norway, July 5—Nine-fifteen P. M., and I am writing without the aid of artificial light. You cannot imagine how beautiful the light is from five to ten P. M.

We are stopping at a quaint hotel where Miss H——— and I have a fine double room for two dollars a day for us both. Breakfast is twenty-seven cents.

July 7—After having my hair marcelled yesterday I put on my best and went to make calls—first on the Foreign Minister, Mr. Christofferson. He said King Haakon VII knew I was coming and if I could wait until another week when the King and Queen would return to Christiania they would receive me, that King Haakon wished to thank me in person for my work for the legation. But I won't be able to wait, much to my sorrow.

I went to see Frau F. Mörck, who is a leading woman here of the Liberal Party now in power. Mr. Christofferson told us the Storthing was now in session and gave me a card to admit me to the diplomatic box. Fr. Mörck went with us, and we sat through a most interesting session from 5:30 to 9 P. M., when the labor bill to limit to ten hours per day was up. They had a lively debate, and the measure was lost by two votes. All the Liberal men disappointed. After the session was over we met several members and were shown all over Parliament House. It is interesting to note the consideration given women because they have the vote.

Later we were taken to the Tea House, where light wines and beer were sold and a band played. We met more people and saw many notables.

The rooms at this house are connected with an open gallery, with flowers on the railing, overlooking a court where a fountain plays. Breakfast is served there.

This is a beautiful city, full of business and very thrifty. Although it is in the latitude of Greenland, it was so warm yesterday that my friend wore a white suit and I my black dress with the new sleeves. But we slept in comfort under a down coverlid and today we are wearing tailored suits again.

Valders, July 9— . . . At six last evening an open barouche drawn by two sturdy little horses came around, and we had a wonderful ride along the lakes in the shadows of the great mountains for two hours to Valders and stopped for the night. Everywhere the fields and roadsides are gay with flowers—buttercups, daisies, bluebells, pansies, wild carrot, and dandelions, and the grass is so green. We have been riding from 7:30 A. M. to 1 P. M. today and are now stopping for dinner. The snow-capped mountain in front of this house is more than five thousand feet high and beyond the lake is a range of mountains mirrored in the clear water.

For dinner we had soup, fresh salmon with butter sauce, potatoes, Norwegian cranberry sauce, larded birds, lettuce salad, whey pudding with wine sauce, and coffee served out of doors.

Laerdal, Norway, July 10—Last night we slept at N——— on the shore of a cold gray lake, and across it were mountains honeycombed with snow banks. Very weary I went to sleep in the dim twilight and slept until 2 A. M. It was daybreak, and yet the moon was mirrored in the peaceful lake. The whole house was light from outdoors. We had a regular Norwegian supper last night. Several kinds of bread, sardines, anchovies, ham, tongue, cold beefsteak, cold sausage, three kinds of cheese, marmalade, salmon trout, hot small sausages, and potatoes, coffee and tea. For breakfast about the same with fresh boiled eggs added. The native cheese, made of goats' milk, is a big square loaf about six inches across and the color of common laundry soap. All the houses are exquisitely clean.

This morning we drove over the highest point, the top of the watershed between Bergen and the east shore. Wonderful! wonderful! Mountains nearly six thousand feet high, and the snow melting and plunging down great waterfalls to the great rocky beds below. There is no way to describe it.

The peasants have taken their cattle and sheep up on the mountains to pasture and they live in little huts with sod roofs on which grass and flowers are growing. The air is fragrant with the sweet red clover and in the yards in the valleys are honeysuckle and lilacs in full bloom.

We met today a gentleman who is going to Russia on his third trip. He says the rumors about cholera are much exaggerated so we may get through after all.

The expenses of this trip are not over five dollars a day, including carriage, hotel, and tips. Bennets mapped out the eleven days and planned ahead everywhere for horses, rooms, and meals and gave us a book of coupons for our cash. So far it works perfectly.

Vossevangen, Norway, July 11, 1909—It is now after eleven o'clock and still light. We started out this morning at 7:30 and rode by steamer on the beautiful Songè fiord and the captain came and spoke to me and showed me his Grand Army button. He was in the Army of the Cumberland for two years. He told me that at Bergen I would see a flag that he took from the Confederates.

Bergen, July 12—We met here the United States Consul, Felix Johnson, and his wife. Last night they took us to a concert in the park. In the fountains there were hundreds of gold fish a foot long.

I have about all the presents I want to buy and also an ermine tippet for myself. It cost less than half what it would in the United States. Of course it is a small piece, but it is real ermine.

July 14—On board the *Vesta*, bound for Molde, Norway. After we got on board we had our first experience in Norway with drunkenness. No officer on the vessel is allowed to drink, but the stewardesses had been drinking and one was boisterous and so they locked her in a stateroom and she behaved very badly until an officer came and locked her up somewhere else. I have learned two Norwegian words: *tak*—thanks, and *ikke*—not. I must describe our breakfast on board steamer this morning. Coffee, bread and butter, beefsteak and onions, stale eggs, four kinds of cheese, cold sausage, tongue, ham, pressed beef, sardines, and marmalade.

It will be three weeks tomorrow since I sailed and last saw all of you. I am homesick for letters and imagine all kinds of things that may have happened to you.

Molde, July 15—This is the loveliest spot I have ever seen. The Moldefiord is in front of us and across is the long range of snow-capped mountains.

July 17— . . . At 4 P. M. we start on a long drive of five hours to B——— to take the boat for Trondhjem. The Norwegians are an industrious people and very clean. I like them very much. Met again at breakfast the man who calls himself Senator W———. He is traveling in an automobile at a cost of $60 a day for the machine. He must have a time getting across the streams. He is a boor, and probably made his money grafting.

Trondhjem, July 18—Our boat was very small with a smelly, musty cabin but "Bennet" had ordered that we have the ladies' salon on the main deck for our exclusive use so our beds were made up on sofas and we spent the night there. The rest of the passengers had to sit out on the cold decks, except two other American women who were assigned to the smoking room. We learned that the regular boat had been taken to transport troops for a few days and this little boat was a substitute.

This is the coldest season for years on this side of the water. I have not really been warm since last Sunday, but we have seen lovely things which we shall always remember. It is 10 P. M. and the sun is still visible above the horizon and the sky is a brilliant orange. I am tired, but it seems a pity to go to bed.

We have our tickets for Stockholm, second class with sleeper—cost, $9.15 in our money, a good deal, it seems, as we leave here at 7:15 tonight and arrive in Stockholm at 8:35 tomorrow evening. This will be my first experience abroad in a sleeper. Had my first hot bath in a big tub since leaving the ship and enjoyed it very much.

July 20, Enroute to Stockholm—At our last station we had seven minutes for lunch. Such a rush, but the coffee was hot and we were so cold. We really like the sleeping arrangements better than those in the United States.

Stockholm, Sweden, Grand Hotel, July 21—It is fine to shed my flannel underwear and begin to thaw out. This is said to be one of the finest hotels on the continent, and we are fortunate to get comfortable single rooms at five kroner, $1.35 a day. This city is called the northern Venice, and it is very beautiful with its many canals and waterways, parks, and substantial public buildings.

July 23—The Consul General is very discouraging about Russia. One man returned from there has been kept in quarantine in Germany for five days and visited every day by a physician. The game would not be worth the candle.

We went to the Palace today and saw the apartments of the King and Queen, but the Council was in session so we did not see the state rooms. Then we went through the old town and met a Swedish girl who spoke to us in good English and said she had lived four years in Washington.

We went into the market and smelled the thirty kinds of cheese and saw strawberries, gooseberries, green peas, and many flowers. For eight cents in our money I bought a pint of strawberries and we made them a part of our supper.

A newspaper woman has asked me for an interview and is going to write me up for the woman's paper of Sweden. The struggles of these women for suffrage are wonderful.

July 24—It seems to rain here almost as easily as in Norway. We went by appointment this morning to see a fine public school building with swimming pool. This afternoon we went out to the Stockholm Industrial Exposition. It is small but wonderful. The world does not know what Sweden can do in industrial art.

I was interviewed this afternoon by a newspaper woman and my picture is to be published.

July 25—This region is beautiful. The foliage is so green and abundant and there are so many castles and villas. We have been to Skansen where we saw many of the folk dances and also old houses, including a Lapp settlement with reindeer.

July 26—We have been today to Upsala, the great Swedish University. Swedenborg is buried there. His remains were brought from

London last year and now the Swedish government is going to put up a handsome memorial to him in the great cathedral.

We were entertained by Mrs. Hegan, wife of one of the professors. She is president of the Woman Suffrage Society of Upsala, numbering two hundred women, and has taught her little girl, Helga, to say in English, "Votes for women." That is all the English the child can say.

We shall be sorry to leave these rooms with running hot water, for we can't have that luxury again I fear.

July 28, on the Gota Canal—This canal is a wonder, the first successful experiment in making water "go up hill." It is now a century old. The cabins on this boat are very tiny, and the berth no wider than my red plush sofa, and I don't know how I shall hang on to it for two nights.

We had at dinner the Swedish "smor" for first course, all cold dishes. On the sideboard are set out bread and butter, cheese, several kinds of fish, dried and spiced, sardines, and crawfish, etc., and you take a plate and help yourself and eat all you want, then after that they bring you soup, fish, meats, and dessert. Today with the "smor" they served a white drink which seemed to be Scotch whisky and anise seed.

We are greatly disappointed about not going to Russia, but the Germans seem to have established a quarantine on account of the cholera.

July 29—We did not have a very comfortable night on account of our narrow berths and the noise. We went through fifteen locks in the night. I had a pleasant walk this morning with a party of Americans, going a mile or so from a lower lock to one some distance above. The farmers are cutting their hay now, using the old-fashioned scythe. It rains so much that they cannot dry hay on the ground so they have long racks about five feet high in the fields and the hay hangs there until it is quite dry. The grass is fine and the cattle are fat. We saw fine vegetable gardens and along the canal are piled cords and cords of wood, mostly white birch. Yesterday was clear and sunny all day, but the rain has come again this morning.

Gottenborg, Sweden, July 31—Our beautiful canal trip is over, and I have that odd sense of comfort at something completed. Last night we reached Trollhattan Falls about 7 o'clock and got out and walked with a tow-headed boy for a guide to see Sweden's largest and finest falls, not much as to power but very picturesque. We paid our guide about seven cents in our money.

Enroute to Copenhagen—My friend again has a sick headache. Too much rich food. Two people got into our compartment and Miss H——— and I talked English in complete unconcern until the lady laughed, and we found she was from Portland, Oregon, and her husband is a Swede bringing her over to see his family.

Copenhagen, Denmark, Aug. 2—Today we went to the "True Church" to see Thorwaldsen's Christ and the Apostles. Wonderful! wonderful!

Aug. 3—We called on Minister Egan, and he was most cordial and begged me to remain over so he could give a dinner in my honor on Thursday. It seems he sent the dining room furniture to the cabinet maker to be fixed and it won't be ready until Thursday. It's quite a temptation to stay over, but I won't yield.

This afternoon we went to Rosenborg Castle, a treasure house of tapestries, china, inlaid tables, carved furniture, rare silver, and brass, decorated ceilings and walls. The grounds are beautiful, too.

Berlin, Germany, Aug. 5—We found that in Germany there is no allowance for baggage but it only cost me about seventy cents for my steamer trunk. Our car was a through one, and when we got to the station we found that although we had a ticket we also had to have a seat reserved before we could go through the gate, but no extra charge. A very good way to be sure of a seat. In our compartment were three gentlemen and ourselves. One of them, we were informed, is an eminent composer, but he was not very tidy so we did not make friends with him; but a big burly Dane we did, and he turned out to be most agreeable. He had been in the States at the time of the Chicago Exposition and he talked a quaint English. He told me he was unmarried and showed evidence of admiring my friend.

I have the dearest room looking out on a garden and on the same floor as the dining room, with a lovely springy couch bed and down coverlid—cost six marks, or $1.50 a day, including meals and everything—and I am going to rest here most of the time until I sail. It is clean and quiet here and they speak English. Frau N——— used to be a teacher in Washington at the Somers School, and many people stop here when in Berlin.

My dearest love to each one of you and a kiss, too. I wish I had money to buy all the pretty things I see for you. Remember me to all inquiring friends.

Berlin, Aug. 6—I have bought the long coat I wanted, a dark blue English heavy serge in diagonal, for about $12 of our money. It would cost double that at home. My hat was a wreck, so I have had it retrimmed and when I get my suit cleaned I shall be quite decent.

Aug. 7—Last night we went to the opera to hear Tannhäuser. It was beautiful. It began at seven, and it seemed so funny to ride to the opera in broad daylight, but it was my first ride through the immense Tiergarten, a perfect forest right in the heart of the city. The opera house is just off the Sieges-Allee, a great avenue lined with statues of the reigning royal family. The Emperor has put up these statues to his ancestors, and one cannot but feel that it is unworthy of him and of them. He is so disliked, but his subjects dare not say so. When they

11

want to speak of him disrespectfully they say "Mr. Johnson is so and so . . ."

Well, this house is American headquarters. Many people come and go that I know.

Sunday, Aug. 8—I am going to church for the first time since I left Washington and it seems nice to look forward to. The Rev. Lyman Abbott will preach at the American church near here.

Yesterday we went to the great Emperor Frederick Museum. It has some of the best specimens of every kind of period art in the principal countries and all beautifully arranged.

It was so warm last night we went to a beautiful garden in the suburbs, with a great fountain in the center that was beautifully illuminated. A fine band was playing. It cost about eight cents in our money to get in but you had to buy refreshments in order to get a table.

We have heard Dr. Lyman Abbott, and he gave us a good sermon on the text, "What does the Lord require of you?" I wonder he can be so bigoted about woman's rights and duties when he is so broad on religious matters. It was pleasant to hear our good old hymns and see only American faces.

I wish Betty could see the flowers here. Just now there are miles and miles of fuchsias in bloom.

Aug. 9—Have just been interviewed by a newspaper woman for the English daily paper published in Dresden. The Berlin women want to entertain me, but I am not going to wait for that.

Aug. 11—On Monday we were all day at Potsdam, the home of the royal family of Prussia. I had no idea how beautiful it was there or how much there was to see. We got a "drosky" for our use, with a jolly driver who had learned to "spiel off" in English. I wish I could picture the old fellow for you as he sat on the box with his back as round as an apple. He took us everywhere and landed us at the railroad station just five minutes before the train to Berlin was due and he was so pleased when we gave him a tip of fifty cents. He told my friend in German a great number of the old scandals about Napoleon and the German royal family.

The town of Potsdam is called the "cradle of the Prussian army." There is a large institution for the orphans of non-commissioned officers, and the garrison consists of the picked men of five regiments. They showed us the measuring rod for these men, and not even the tallest man in our party going through the palace was up to the requirements.

I think the grounds around the palace are the best part, wonderful effects in landscape gardening and of course centuries of care must tell.

The new palace, the summer residence of the Emperor, is positively ugly both outside and in. There is one immense room decorated with shells and minerals, etc. It may suit the German taste but oh! my . . .

We have been to see the new cathedral as an evidence of the Emperor's taste and it also is ugly, but the stained glass windows are fine.

Last night we went to the opera, Lohengrin. Between acts we walked in the garden as is the custom.

Aug. 12—This afternoon we took a long walk in the Tiergarten. In the old time it was the Emperor's hunting forest, then a deer park, and now, although it is still the private property of the crown, it is open to the public. In one place we saw about a quarter of an acre in sand and hundreds of children playing in it. There are many fine statues in the park and quiet walks and pleasant seats, also a fine road for horseback riding.

Aug. 13—This morning we went to the National Gallery, which has a fine collection of paintings by modern artists. We were there over three hours. The Barbizon school is particularly well represented by Millet, Daubigny, and Constable, and there is also a very complete collection of paintings and drawings by the most famous German artists, including some immense cartoons. We saw Canova's "Hebe." It has a brass cup instead of a marble one.

This morning when I came in to breakfast Mr. H——— began to tease me about the half column notice about me in the *Daily Record.* I am pinning it to this sheet and want it saved for the scrap book.

Aug. 14—Am packed up except my things from the laundry promised to be done last night, then this morning at eleven. It is now eleven thirty so you see laundresses are the same the world over.

So far I have not found any lace that I wanted at a reasonable price, so I looked at ostrich feathers and found they were about half the price we pay at home.

Dresden, Aug. 15—I am charmed with Dresden. Miss H——— and I are like little girls about a new place and after supper last night we went out and walked until the shops were all dark. This morning we were at the great picture gallery until we had to come back to dinner. It was a fine dinner and included smothered chicken and chocolate ice cream. This is a free day at the gallery, and it was crowded. The world-famous Sistine Madonna is here and is quite as beautiful and satisfying as I expected. We did not get through the first floor today and will go again.

Aug. 18—On Monday we went for the day to Saxon, Switzerland, leaving here by rail and reaching the town of Potzscha where we were ferried across the beautiful Elbe river to the quaint little town of Wehlen. After much haggling we got a drosky to take us up to the top of the Bastei, a wonderful rock formation from which there is a sheer drop of over 600 feet down to the river. From the heights we could see off into Bohemia. It is sublime. The day turned quite warm, but we were game and pursued our itinerary of walking down the more than 600 steps to a picturesque restaurant for dinner. A man served us who was as round as a bolster and about six times as big. The views on every side were beautiful, and the people interesting.

Then we took a boat back to Dresden. Oh! how my knees still ache. I have had to wear old shoes ever since, but it was worth it. A couple of men who passed us as we came down those interminable slippery steps said in German, "Gee, see those American ladies sweat." We tumbled into our beds as soon as supper was over.

This morning we have been to the Green Vault in the "Schloss" and have seen the wonderful ivories and jewels, great necklaces of diamonds, including the famous green diamond, and rubies, and pearls, etc. Then we went to the lovely porcelain museum, and on our way back I bought the last Christmas present; so you may all understand that your presents are in my little steamer trunk and it is too late to hint as to any choice you might have.

Since I have been in Germany I have been more than ever distressed to see women such beasts of burden. I have seen nice-looking, decently dressed women in the thills, drawing heavy carts, and in the country, pregnant women and poor old women bent almost double under heavy burdens of wood. In restaurants the man will sit down first, leaving his wife to get a seat as she can. He will take off his hat in profound obeisance to another man but not to his wife. "I, a lord of creation, salute you, another lord of creation," it seems. They always treat American women with respect.

Tomorrow morning I start for Antwerp and I hate to leave Miss Hartmann who has been so kind and such a willing interpreter. I don't know how I shall get along by myself, but there is to be a dining car out, and the coaches are to be vestibule coaches, which means all modern conveniences. I feel as if my vacation were about over when I turn my face homeward, and I should be glad to go swiftly in an air car. But it will soon be over and I shall be back at work. Well, I can frivol and I can work, but I refuse to grow old.

Ellen S. Mussey.

Chapter XVIII

A CONVERT TO THE SUFFRAGE CAUSE

From the time she had first come to Washington Mrs. Mussey had been associated with women suffragists, and she thought that women should have the right to vote, yet she had taken no part whatever in activities to gain the vote. She had simply been indifferent to this struggle.

Not until 1896 had she felt the slightest quickening on the subject. Lobbying for her bill to give the mother the same rights as the father in the child, Mrs. Mussey had had her first glimpse of the real value of the ballot when Senator Warren, of Wyoming, had said, "I believe in your bill but if I didn't, I'd have to vote for it because I'm here through women's votes." She had wished then that all congressmen were under obligation to women constituents. But her bill had been passed and her attitude toward the suffrage question had become passive again.

The visit to Norway and Sweden in 1909, however, was both enlightening and stimulating. In Norway women had the vote, and because of it, members of the Storthing were giving women consideration that was entirely unknown in the United States. Mrs. Mussey was profoundly impressed. And in Sweden, where women did not have the vote, she was brought face to face with their stupendous struggle to get the ballot. Everywhere women were talking suffrage and everywhere they asked her about the progress being made in the United States.

They took it for granted that a woman who practiced law before the Supreme Court of the United States, a woman who was responsible for reform legislation in behalf of women, and who was the dean of a law school, must necessarily be vitally interested in the suffrage movement.

And it was the attitude of these foreign women that finally stirred Ellen Spencer Mussey to action. Upon her return home she at once allied herself with the National American Woman Suffrage Association, and in 1910 she went before a committee of the Senate to make a plea for the ballot. At this hearing were Dr. Anna Howard Shaw and Dr. Anna Hamilton.

But woman suffrage was not favored by the Senate. The chairman of the Senate committee on woman suffrage, Mr. Bacon, of Georgia, complimented Mrs. Mussey on her arguments but he showed no sign of helping with the necessary legislation. The President, William Howard Taft, was totally opposed to enfranchising women, and the fight loomed as a long and arduous one. But throughout the country women were organizing and were making their demands more urgent. Suffrage meetings were being held everywhere, and Mrs. Mussey spoke at many of these on the Pacific Coast in the summer of 1911 when she went to California as a delegate to a meeting of the National Education Association.

She attended to legal work on this journey and also visited scenic points in the west. Miss Wilhelmina Hartman accompanied her. As was her custom, Mrs. Mussey kept her family informed of her experiences.

Salt Lake City, July 1, 1911—I am waiting at the hotel for a hearing "in chambers" by the court. It is a Swedish case, and my local attorney does not seem to be able to convince the judge, so he is trying to get a special hearing for me this afternoon.

Friday we came within sight of the mountains of Wyoming, strange weird things, so barren and with such peculiar outlines. Miss H——— was carsick and confined to her berth all the way. She ate nothing after leaving Chicago until just before we reached Salt Lake but is as cheery as ever in spite of it. I would never have the courage to travel if I was afflicted like that.

This morning I took in the town on a "Seeing Salt Lake" auto. It was very interesting. Then I went to the tabernacle and heard the great organ and a sermon on Mormonism. How I would like to see you all today, but it is lovely not to hear the telephone and to be out of business for a while. . . .

Old Faithful, Yellowstone Park, July 3—I wish I could share with you the pleasures of this day. The air is so fine and bracing and sweet with balsam. We rode twenty-nine miles by coach and have seen about thirty geysers in action. This hotel is in the best rustic style even to furnishings. There is a big fire in the open fire place in the central hall, the heat is turned on in the bedrooms, and I have on my winter underwear.

Yellowstone Lake, July 4—Just think, this is the Fourth of July and we had a game of snowball when we stopped at a wayside spring for a cooling drink. We rode thirty-six miles today, crossing the continental divide twice and reaching an altitude of 8000 feet and winding around and around corkscrew roads. We have seen ranges of snow-capped mountains all day.

My face is badly burned and the mosquitoes are great pests, but this hotel is well screened so I guess I can sleep.

The Grand Canyon of the Yellowstone, July 5—The canyon is gorgeous in yellows, blacks, gray, all shades of brown, and red, and bits of pines grow in the rocks. All that is needed are a few Indians in paint and feathers to make the picture complete.

This is a new hotel, not yet completed. It is four stories, with elevators, electric lights, the latest plumbing, and every luxury known to the modern hotel. The bell boys are all college boys, earning some money and getting experience.

Last night a man went out to walk at the Lake House and stepped in a hot hole and had to be taken to the infirmary. Did I tell you that I saw a big silver bear? Last evening a big mother bear and two cubs came out and made demonstrations which frightened two boys and a lady in a hobble skirt. Even the soldier on guard was pale, they said, and drew his pistol, etc., etc. Of course the boys are very happy over the experience.

Later—After dinner we went out to see the sights, and two deer and a little fawn came down to drink at a stream near the hotel.

I am writing in the lounge, a fine string band is playing, and about two hundred guests are in the big room, some writing, some playing cards, and some listening. I am tired and must go to bed for we start at eight tomorrow morning for a thirty-five-mile drive to Mammoth, and on Friday we have to drive forty-seven miles to take the train for Ogden.

Mammoth Hot Springs, July 6—We have seen the geysers at Norris Basin. They cover several acres and are hot steam and mud, and one of them just growls and growls but does nothing. We had to walk on boards over this basin with warning signs of "danger" on every hand. This is where President Roosevelt entered the park on his visit several years ago. The air is dry and very exhilarating. The wild flowers are wonderfully fine. I am sending Betty a few of them. I hope that you are all well.

San Francisco, July 15—I have just come from the woman's suffrage meeting at the Palace Hotel where I spoke to a fine audience and was afterward guest of honor at a tea at the hotel.

I dressed in my white serge suit with my white lace hat and big ostrich feather. I had a big bouquet of sweet peas (pink) which cost me fifteen cents. In Washington they would have been at least seventy-five.

Next Saturday I am to be a guest at a big suffrage luncheon at Berkeley when I return from Yosemite.

The Yosemite, July 18, 1911—At last, I am realizing my lifelong wish to camp in the Sierras. I meant to come to this country before I was married, but General Mussey kept me on the Atlantic coast.

It was a hot ride by rail to El Portal, and the hotel at that point is one of the hottest places you can imagine. I had to bind a wet towel around my head in order to sleep at all. But the sixteen miles here by coach were cool and beautiful. The road is along the Merced River and canyon. We saw the great waterfalls over 2600 feet plunge. Just think of that! Camp Curry is a real camp, and I like it so much that Miss H——— has consented to spend an extra day here. We each have a tent to ourselves, with spring bed, bureau, washstand, and rocking chair. Fine spring water is piped all over the grounds. Our back fence is Sentinel Rock. The people are very sociable and many of them dress for tramping in khaki suits. I have never seen such great grand trees.

I must tell you about the camp fires. In the center of the camp, which is recarpeted every Sunday morning with fragrant pine needles, is a flat platform of big stones, and in the center of that an upright iron frame to hold pine logs. All the papers are picked up on the grounds and put in boxes and set on this platform. Then pine logs are set on top of that and in the evening the fire is lighted. Two or three hundred people sit about in steamer chairs and other chairs.

Mr. Curry has the voice of a trumpeter and he gives information about the trips and country round about. Glacier Point is just back of the camp, a sheer cliff three-fourths of a mile high. Nearly every night people are up there from the camp, and they build a fire and throw down the burning brands. The falling fire is one of the sights of the place.

Then an organ is pulled out on the porch and some one leads in old songs like "Tenting Tonight."

Miss H——— has gone on for an extra trip to Wawona, where the big redwoods are. It is nearly sixty miles hard staging, and I did not think it wise to take such a fatiguing trip. The trees in Yosemite are giants. I have never seen such yellow pines.

San Francisco, July 22, 1911—Found all my home letters and was rejoiced to know you are all well.

Went today to a big suffrage luncheon at Berkeley. A fine enthusiastic body of women. They are conducting their campaign with great vigor. Margaret Haley, of Chicago, told of the teachers' fight for increased pay and their war on the corporations to make them pay their taxes. She is very petite and a born Irish fighter. These Chicago teachers hold that women have a right to teach after they are married and should be as free to pursue their loved profession as a man.

I had so much business mail today that I had to have a stenographer .

July 26—Last Sunday Mr. McK——— took me up on the beautiful Russian River where Mrs. McK——— has a bungalow. She was glad to see me, and I enjoyed it very much. On Monday morning we went down to their old home at Santa Rosa, and Mr. McK——— got a fine team and took us all over the town and surrounding country. We drove out to Burbank's place and saw his experimental garden, including his spineless cactus, and we also met Mr. Burbank himself. He talked with us and paid me a very fine compliment as a "woman who did things."

Yesterday there were memorial services in Union Square in honor of Mrs. Sargent, who was a great suffrage leader and the widow of Senator Sargent. It was very impressive. We had fine talks from men and women and sang some national airs. No funeral business at all.

Shasta Springs, Calif., July 30—This is a glorious place with great snow-capped Mt. Shasta in full view. The springs are a sparkling soda water and most trains stop for passengers to sample the tipple.

On Thursday we were guests of Mrs. P———, meeting her at Palo Alto, and we rode in her auto for twenty-five miles through the great San Jose and Santa Clara fruit valley. Miles of orchards of apricots and acres covered with the fruit, drying in trays. Great orchards of prunes, almonds, and peaches—a wonderful sight. They have no rain here from early May until fall and a very even temperature.

Afterward we drove around Stanford University. It gives a very good idea of the damage done by the earthquake five years ago.

On Saturday I attended to a law case in San Francisco, and Mrs. McK——— gave a luncheon and later a tea in my honor. I was pretty tired when I got on the train, but three men had my section and would not even give me a seat. The railroad had sold my berth twice. I finally got another lower berth, but not until I had said some things.

Steamer Jefferson, enroute to Alaska, Aug. 9, 1911—Well, I am really on my way to the Alaska I have dreamed of so long. After looking the ground over, Miss H——— and I decided this was the very best vessel, and we have the bridal chamber. What do you think of that? It is so roomy that we have two windows, two chairs, and a table, as well as the regular berths. But a very antiquated toilet arrangement. Also I have the unexpected luxury of a warm sea bath every morning just as you have on a regular voyage.

Our most distinguished fellow passenger is Jim Jeffries. He and his brother are on their way to Alaska for a four-months' hunting trip. It is strange to see young ladies of apparently good social standing seeking the honor of an introduction. Of course all the broken-down clergymen on board are interviewing him—to make material for sermons, I suppose. He has immense hands, a small nose, ears that stand out from his head, and a good clear eye. He is a big hulking fellow.

We came through Seymour Narrows yesterday about four o'clock. This is the most dangerous point on the trip and is where the *Spokane* went down. Our Captain Wood is one of the famous navigators of this coast and also a fine dancer. All of the crew are Scandinavian except the first mate, and he is Irish.

It is very damp and we are afraid it may rain. The near shore is wooded with low pines but back of them are ranges of snow-capped mountains. So far the Indian villages are not at all picturesque. Just plain white wooden houses. We expect to make our first landing tomorrow at a place whose name begins with a K and sounds like a sneeze.

Ketchikan, Aug. 10—I put my foot on Alaskan soil at nine this morning at this odd place where there are great salmon canneries. There was a landing at six this morning in the cold fog at Metlakatla, where Mr. Duncan has done such wonderful missionary work among the Indians, but I refused to get up at that hour in the cold for any Indians, no matter how good. I saw the little village from my cabin window and Mr. Duncan, a very venerable figure, came down to the wharf.

We landed here after breakfast and the purser and Jim Jeffries led us up the creek to see the salmon. They are fighting up the rapids to fresh water to spawn and they are so thick that several of the passengers caught them in their hands. After the salmon spawn, they gradually decay until there is nothing left but heads and bones.

We walked about two miles up the creek and saw the gorge, rapids, and lovely evergreens. Then we came back and saw a typical Alaskan town, hotels, bars, restaurants, dogs, postal cards, and curio shops. One woman was wild to see Jim Jeffries—said she had never seen a notorious man before.

Beyond Ketchikan—The fog has lifted and we are in fairy land. It is finer than Norway. Such ranges of snow-capped mountains, such glaciers, such reflections, such a wonderful sky! If only you could see it. It is cold at night but by noon it is warm enough to be comfortable.

There is a little Alaskan Indian on board with his guardian, a missionary lady. They say he had a scrap with the other boys on board and whipped them soundly.

Wrangell, Aug. 11—Wrangell is one of the oldest towns in Alaska, and we saw totem poles, one of them with an immense green frog near the top. The town is very picturesquely situated but is dilapidated and forlorn. When the boom was on, they tell me, six and seven thousand people were housed here. Now there is less than a thousand, and part of the houses have been burned.

I am living outdoors so much I am brown as a berry and eat four meals a day.

Fort Haines, Alaska, Aug. 12—Yesterday we saw the great and beautiful Taku Glacier. It cleared up very bright, and we sailed up right in front of it, all light and honeycombed with wonderful blues and greens and little caves and great fissures. Three times great bergs broke off and came into the sea with a vast booming. All around our ship were little floating icebergs.

When we got to Juneau the "Juneau Infants," the boys' baseball team, were at the dock to see big Jim. We just floated around in the wake of the crowd so eager to see the prize fighter.

Miss H——— and I walked up to the old log church and then, seeing the state house and near it a residence with the United States flag flying over it, decided it must be the Governor's residence. We asked a passing resident the name of the Governor, and when he said Clarke, I remembered that ———'s chum was the Governor of this rich territory. Of course we went to see him, and the Governor himself met me at the door and said, "This is Mrs. Mussey, I'm so glad to see you." Then he put us in his private office while he attended to the license to shoot moose which Jim J. wanted. It costs $200 to shoot two moose. We had a fine visit and on our return trip are to come to dinner.

We saw a pretty little Greek church and after dinner went over the great Treadwell mines. They showed us "Old Glory Hole," from which $14,000,000 have been taken.

When the light faded away last night in a wonderful sunset it was ten o'clock and the rosy hues fell on ranges of snow-capped mountains.

After breakfast this morning we visited Fort Seward and saw guard mount. We also saw the Davidson Glacier. It looked dead in comparison to Taku.

This scenery is more beautiful and majestic than in Norway. And we are so thankful for fine weather.

Aug. 14—On Saturday we arrived at Skagway, our most northerly point. Such beautiful lights and shadows and reflections and daylight until 10 P. M. We went by rail up to the Yukon Territory and stopped at Lake Bennett. Here in 1898 was a city of thousands; now there is a half-finished deserted church and an eating house.

All along the way we saw the trail made in 1897-98 by men bound for the Klondike and gold. What hardships they endured and how few came back with gold! The trail is strewn with the whitening bones of pack mules and horses that perished under their burdens.

There is one woman in our party who walked the trail for 150 miles, "Diamond Meg," famous for carrying her diamonds in her teeth, said to have made a fortune keeping an eating house in Bennett. They said she would never get out with her fortune but she did.

Saturday evening we sailed away to Sitka. It is a quaint old Russian town. First we rode in a gay red wagon to the park and saw the totem poles that have been erected along the road in memory of certain chiefs.

Another point of interest is Baranoff Rock where the Russian commander used to "retire to meditate," says the guide book, but native tradition says he rested there when drunk.

Here is the Indian mission school named for the Rev. Sheldon Jackson, who endowed it in his will. The students do all the work and learn trades and domestic arts. The Alaskan Indian does not look like other Indians and the United States Superintendent of Education in Southeastern Alaska, whom I met, says they take readily to civilization.

I shall never forget these glorious sunsets over the snow-capped mountains. This morning we have the clearest day of all and can see points not usually visible.

Just stopped at a little post to take on salmon, and such a stench!

At every stopping place the first thing we see is a procession of squaws coming down with their bundle of wares, baskets, moccasins, and totem poles, but they won't sell anything at a reasonable price so I have not bought anything.

Aug. 16—Last evening we stopped at Ketchikan and loaded salmon for twelve hours. Such a noise all night, but I managed to sleep some. This morning we made our last stop and loaded on 8000 cases of salmon.

As a result of the stop at Ketchikan the stewards got drunk and one, he who had charge of the baths, got left. Captain Wood is an exception to the general run of sea captains and rarely swears, but the men were so slow in loading that he let loose this morning and roared and swore with the worst of them.

We had only an hour on our return stop at Juneau so I didn't dine with Governor Clarke, but he came down to the boat.

Well, Alaska is behind us now and we are just off some islands belonging to British Columbia. I will be in Washington Sept. 3. I long to see you all.

Ellen S. Mussey.

Chapter XIX

CAMPAIGNS

In 1906 the District of Columbia established its first Juvenile Court and the President appointed a man as judge. But certain women of the bar objected. They believed the Juvenile Court should be presided over by a woman, and when the term of office expired in 1912, they campaigned for the appointment of a woman. Their candidate was Ellen Spencer Mussey.

The public was startled. A woman as judge . . . Impossible! Tongues were loosed in ridicule and masculine wits caricatured the lady's hat in the ring, mocked at addressing a judge as "your honoress," and were caustic in their comments regarding the ability of any woman to handle cases involving boys. Some admitted that it might be all right to have a woman preside over cases concerning girls and they suggested the court have two branches, one for boys and one for girls.

A few, however, believed that Mrs. Mussey was unusually well qualified to look after boys as well as girls and they backed her candidacy. But they could not overcome the great mass of public opinion. Besides, the President, William H. Taft, scorned the idea of women in office.

Mrs. Mussey, therefore, was not appointed. But her campaign had accomplished something. The opening wedge had been inserted; the first rude shock of something new had passed; and the public was being prepared to accept a woman on the bench in the future, just as now it accepted women of the law.

An amendment to grant women the vote, drafted by Susan B. Anthony, had been introduced in Congress for the first time in 1878. And every year women had held meetings and pleaded before Congressional committees for favorable action on this amendment. But the majority of the lawmakers believed that women should not have the vote and that most of them did not want it. It was feared that the ballot in the hands of women would become a dangerous weapon.

A new century was ushered in and still women, save those of a few western states, were denied enfranchisement. It became evident that meetings and pleas were without effect, that more spectacular measures must be used to open the eyes of the nation to women's demands. They began to hold suffrage parades. In huge numbers they gathered in cities throughout the country, girded on the glowing yellow suffrage colors, carried aloft the suffrage banners, and marched through the principal streets.

A magnificent parade was planned for Washington, D. C. With strategy, too. It was to be held March 3, 1913, the day before Woodrow Wilson was to be inaugurated as President, the first Democrat in twenty years to attain this high office. Thousands would come to the national capital to celebrate this victory. And thousands would witness the demonstration for woman suffrage.

It was necessary to have a permit to parade, and a committee of women went to the Chief of Police, Major Sylvester, to get his official sanction. But Major Sylvester was opposed to women suffragists and he refused to grant them police protection for any such demonstration. The women sought help of the District Commissioners. And the Commissioners at once urged them to give up the project for it would be foolhardy, they said, to try to parade without the full protection of the police.

But Alice Paul, chairman of the Congressional Committee of the Suffrage Association, who was in charge of the proposed parade, had taken militant part in suffrage activities in England and she was not easily dissuaded or frightened. She declared that the women must parade. And Mrs. Mussey, who was to head the delegation of women of the law, agreed with Miss Paul.

"Women are taxpayers as well as men," said Mrs. Mussey, "and since men taxpayers have been parading all these years, women have a right to do likewise."

Mrs. Mussey in the Suffrage Campaigns.

It was suggested then by various officials that the women march on Sixteenth street, a thoroughfare stretching north from the White House, in a district of embassies and residences, a nice ladylike part of the city. They would be safe there.

But the suffragists knew that no one would see them on Sixteenth Street; that Pennsylvania Avenue was the only place to parade for all Washington parades were held there. They asked the help of a committee of the Senate. Some of the senators were doubtful about the advisability of a suffrage parade. Senator Works, of California, remarked that in the west women would be perfectly safe in holding such a demonstration, but he was worried about what the reaction might be among certain classes of men in the east.

At last, though, a permit to parade was granted, and the Chief of Police was instructed to provide adequate protection.

Ten thousand women from all walks of life—physicians, lawyers, teachers, actresses, dancers, musicians, bookkeepers, stenographers, tradeswomen, and housekeepers—gathered on Capitol Hill. They dressed in costume, many of them wearing the brilliant suffrage colors. There were yellow dresses, yellow hat trimmings, amber beads, and bouquets of jonquils. And there were the golden suffrage banners with their pungent mottoes. The Capitol Plaza glowed.

Bands played. And, preceded by a herald, Inez Milholland, riding a magnificent white horse, the suffragists started five abreast down Capitol Hill toward the Avenue. Their eyes were alight, their steps purposeful, they were making history, emblazoning before the world the demand for their rights, the first woman suffragists to march on this world-famous thoroughfare.

The avenue was thronged with spectators, some who sympathized with the cause, some who were merely curious, and many who bitterly opposed votes for women. At the very foot of Capitol Hill a surging ugly mob waited.

The first group of suffragists set foot upon the avenue, and this mob, jeering and shouting obscenities, closed in upon them. Tawdry denizens of the "Division," Washington's notorious red-light district, joined drunken men in hurling epithets at the suffragists.

Mrs. Mussey, gray-haired and sixty-three, led the division of lawyers, and the rabble, catching sight of her, gave itself up to making coarse jokes about the "old grandma." They pressed against her so that she could not walk.

Glimpsing a policeman in the crowd, Mrs. Mussey cried out to him for help. But the policeman only laughed at her. He made not the slightest move toward restoring order or clearing the line of march.

Battling with all their strength, the women fought their way, sometimes two abreast, sometimes singly, through the rioting masses. Sometimes for fifteen or twenty minutes they could make no advancement whatever.

Boy scouts, true to their training, bravely took a hand and tried to force the mob back to the curb, but their efforts were unavailing. All along the line of march were policemen, too, but they merely looked on while pandemonium reigned. For nearly two hours the rioting continued unabated.

At last a call for help reached the Secretary of War, and soldiers from Fort Myer across the Potomac were rushed to Washington. Then the rioters were quelled, the avenue cleared, and the women finished their parade.

But Washington was in disgrace. News of the abuse of the suffragists was flashed about the country. Bitter denunciation was heard on every hand. And Congress began an investigation. The Chief of Police was called to an accounting and, though it was noised about that he had told his men the suffragists did not deserve protection, though it was plain no effort had been made to keep order, he was ready with excuses. But when the investigation ended the Chief of Police was quietly removed from his post.

For the suffragists, however, the parade was a notable victory. Maltreatment at the hands of the crowds and the police energized the cause, and scores of people who had been wholly indifferent now turned their attention to winning the vote for women.

But Mrs. Mussey paid dearly for her part in the parade. For a long time she had not been well, her strength was slowly being exhausted by too many activities, and the ordeal with the rioters exacted a final toll. She became seriously ill. For weeks she lay unconscious with no hope held out for her recovery.

There were so many things to live for, however, so much work still to be done. And after a long rest, the spark of life began to glow again.

But recuperation was slow. It would be a long time before she could resume her duties again and she resigned as dean of the law school. The Board of Trustees appointed Miss Gillett dean, and Mrs. Mussey, because of her long service, was made honorary dean for life.

The college was growing rapidly now. It boasted one hundred fifty students, with a freshman class of fifty-five. And, though the problem of housing the school grew more acute each year and the financial situation continued to be precarious, one phase of the school's development thoroughly amazed its founders.

In spite of the fact that they had made their college co-educational, they had not expected any great number of men students, and had supposed that a school founded primarily for women would remain predominantly a woman's school. But early in its history men had begun to enroll, and now half the student body was composed of men. Mrs. Mussey and Miss Gillett could hardly believe their eyes or even the school records.

Because of the personnel of the teaching staff and the low tuition, however, men were quick to take advantage of this school, and it became increasingly evident that the old argument that men would not study law in the same classes with women had had no basis whatever in fact, but was a mere figment of prejudiced minds.

Brothers came to the school with their sisters, husbands with wives, fathers with daughters, and sons with mothers. In 1914 Mrs. Sarah T. Andrew and her son, Herbert B. Andrew, were graduated in the same class and were hailed as the first mother and son ever to be graduated together from a law school. Later, Mrs. Andrew's husband, not to be outdone by his wife and son, became a student at the college. Progress!

And another hoary argument, that long treasured one, that women had not the mentality for the law, was being constantly refuted. For more and more women were going into active practice and more and more of them were being given responsible positions with the government. Naturally, too, more and more women were seeking an education in the law.

It took a long time, however, for the full realization of this to dawn upon those Washington law schools that had been so adamant regarding the admission of women. Perhaps it was the pinch of competition that finally helped their understanding; or perhaps, sensing the bigness of true reform, they wanted a share in it. At any rate, in 1912 the law school of George Washington University, formerly Columbian College, opened its doors to women, and a few years later the National University began to admit women to its law courses.

Yet in some communities a woman of the law was still a rarity, was still looked upon with amazement, and some of them still felt it necessary to use their initials to disguise somewhat the fact that they were women. Mrs. Sarah T. Andrews, practicing law in the District of Columbia after her graduation in 1914, followed this plan when she had a case at Frederick, Maryland. Though Maryland admitted women to the bar, few women practiced law there, and Mrs. Andrew, going to Frederick for final hearings of her case after having conducted the preliminary work by correspondence under the name S. T. Andrew, caused a considerable stir.

Indeed, so unusual was the occasion of a woman appearing at this bar of justice that a visitor to the court, a wealthy, outstanding character of the community, came up and asked Mrs. Andrew for the privilege of shaking hands with her.

"I just want to say this," he exclaimed as he grasped her hand vigorously, "I've rid in a Packard car going eighty miles an hour; I've been all through a submarine over on the bay; and I've seen a whole flock of airyplanes; but never till this day did I see a she-lawyer."

At this same time certain states, among them Arkansas, Delaware, Georgia, and Virginia, still were denying women the right of admission to the bar. But there was agitation in Georgia for a more liberal policy. Georgia women, forced for so many years to go elsewhere to study law or to practice law, were seeking that right at home. Many of them had gone to Washington, D. C., and one young woman, Miss Laura M. Berrien, of Waynesboro, Georgia, who attended the school founded by Mrs. Mussey and Miss Gillett, was graduated with the highest honors in her class.

Accounts of her achievements were published in Georgia newspapers and editorials pointed with ridicule to the law that prevented such a talented young woman from being admitted to the bar in her home state. Her story became one of the chief weapons of campaigners urging passage of a bill before the legislature. Miss Berrien, herself, lobbied for the measure.

One congressman whom she interviewed was horrified that she should wish to be a lawyer. "The idea," he cried, "what business has a woman like you to practice law? Why don't you get married?"

Miss Berrien was attractive, and this man could not believe that she would choose to remain single, and the possibility that she might marry and be a lawyer too was wholly beyond his conception.

Certain others, also, thought that the business of women was to get married and not be lawyers. The question was discussed at a meeting of the Georgia Bar Association, and one thoughtful member asked, "What about those women who never marry—should they not have a chance to work at the law if they choose that way to make a living?" But an opponent replied emphatically, "No! if a woman hasn't a husband, let her put in all her time getting one."

The majority, however, held more advanced views, and in 1916 Georgia passed a law giving women the right of admission to the bar. And because Miss Berrien's law school record had figured so importantly in the accomplishment of this reform, Governor N. E. Harris gave her the pen with which he signed the new measure. Very soon, upon special invitation, Miss Berrien was admitted to the bar in Atlanta.

Women suffragists, shortly after their parade on Pennsylvania Avenue in 1913, sent a deputation to the new President, Woodrow Wilson, to ask his support of the national suffrage amendment. But in spite of the fact that this question had long been agitated, was of such vital import to half the population and consequently to all the population, Mr. Wilson said he had not given it any thought. He promised, however, that it would receive his most careful consideration.

Later other deputations visited Mr. Wilson, and he conveyed the idea that he had been so occupied with really paramount issues such as the currency and the tariff that he had had no time to think of woman suffrage or to make mention of it in his message to Congress. But oddly enough he had had time to recommend self government for Filipino men.

Still other delegations went to the President. And they carried petitions to Congress, held hearings, lobbied persistently—all to no avail. President and congressmen were adept at evasions. Politely, beautifully, and sometimes even enthusiastically, they promised the women—nothing. Finally, the President said that the suffrage question was in reality a matter to be settled by the states and not by the National Government. It was evident that he had no intention of supporting the suffrage amendment, that he had no interest in the cause of women. Very likely it annoyed him that women should have a cause.

Mrs. Mussey, back in the fray again as soon as her health would permit, had her first acquaintance with President Wilson and his attitude toward women when he and Mrs. Wilson received the members of the executive board of the National Council of Women. The President was bored. Extremely so. Never would Mrs. Mussey forget her presentation to him and Mrs. Wilson. The Council President, Mrs. Kate Waller Barrett, in introducing Mrs. Mussey, spoke warmly of her achievements, of the founding of the law school, and the legislative work. And Mrs. Wilson greeted Mrs. Mussey with glowing enthusiasm. The President, however, merely looked more bored. Such activities held no interest for him, it seemed. He wished possibly that such women would let him alone. But they didn't.

Suffragists sent to the White House and the Capitol larger and larger deputations, petitions ponderous with names, and they dramatized their demands with larger and larger processions. Yet the suffrage amendment was not passed. And it was nearly forty years since it had first been introduced in Congress. Certain suffragists were in a ferment. It was time for more drastic action they decided; it was time for militancy.

In January, 1917, these suffragists began to picket the White House. Day after day, through rain and snow and icy winds, they stood at the gates of the Executive Mansion and displayed their trenchant banners, demanding, "Mr. President! How long must women wait for liberty?"

This was shocking. Condemnation came thick and fast. In the press the action was characterized as "unwomanly" and "dangerous." Some of the suffragists themselves—the conservatives—strongly disapproved.

The war came. At once government officials, high and low, and men and women throughout the country, urged all suffragists to give up their fight for the vote and turn their attention to helping their country win the war. If they would be nice little girls and do this, the nation out of sheer gratitude would reward them with the vote as soon as the war ended.

But suffragists knew that women had abandoned their cause during the Civil War to help free the Negro and that when they had asked for the vote along with the Negro they had been told, "This is the Negro's hour, women must wait."

And after all these years of waiting the government had the audacity to ask them to keep on waiting, to give their services in still another war, a war for world democracy while they themselves were denied democracy. The absurdity of that!

Assuredly they would not give up the struggle for the vote now. The militant suffragists, organized into the National Woman's Party under the leadership of Alice Paul, became even more spectacular in their fight. They continued to picket the White House and they picketed the Capitol. They carried banners emblazoned with "Democracy should begin at home," "We demand justice and self-government in our own land," "Russia and England are enfranchising their women in war time. How long must American women wait for liberty?"

Conservative suffragists were appalled at these methods. To them such tactics were little less than treasonable. Yet they themselves had no intention of giving up the struggle for the vote, and they continued to work quietly and tirelessly as before to educate the public in the matter of women's rights. Mrs. Mussey belonged to this conservative group. She hotly protested any action that cast reflection upon her country and she not only believed the militant program was harmful to the nation in its prosecution of the war but that it was ruinous to the suffrage cause.

Nevertheless the "militants" continued their sensational acts; they continued to ridicule the government's inconsistencies. And ridicule was painful. Officials took action, and militant suffragists were arrested and fined.

But the fines were not paid. And the women were sent to jail. The story of their incarceration read like something from the dark ages. They were subjected to the most abominable brutality and cruelty; they were knocked down and thrown about as if they were so many sacks of meal; they were vilely threatened; bullied; tortured. Yet they were not subdued. They went on hunger strikes. They kept the suffrage question white hot. It rivalled even the war news.

Picketing was continued with still more startling banners, followed by more arrests, more jail sentences, and more hunger strikes. Militant suffragists were indomitable.

And for that matter so were the conservative suffrage forces. Both factions in their own way fought unceasingly. They canvassed the country, rallying more and more women and men to the cause; they campaigned against congressmen who opposed suffrage, bringing defeat to many a stubborn legislator; they lobbied; they struggled against stupidity, insincerity, double crossing; they combatted anti-suffrage groups, backed by powerful monied interests; they used every weapon at their command and battled simultaneously along every front.

Results were soon evident. On January 10, 1918, the Suffrage Amendment was approved by the House, exactly forty years after it had first been introduced. But the Senate refused to act. Later, October 1, 1918, when it did act, the amendment was lost by two votes.

Again and again the Senate defeated the amendment by this small margin. But the House remained favorable. And by this time millions of women were demanding the vote. Furthermore, women in Europe were actually getting it. Not only England and Russia, but Hungary, Austria, and Germany had enfranchised women.

Finally the United States Senate, through continued pressure and strategy, capitulated. At a special session in May, 1919, the House again acted favorably on the Suffrage Amendment, and in June the Senate passed it with a vote of 66 to 30.

Next came the arduous campaigns for ratification by the states. Anti-suffrage forces were on every hand to block adoption. Absurd and maddening obstacles were raised. And only after the most heartbreaking efforts, the most adept political maneuvering, was the last necessary thirty-sixth state won. Tennessee ratified the amendment in 1920, and women at last had the vote.

Militant suffragists claimed the victory. They pointed proudly to results following two years of militancy as opposed to the acomplishments in forty years of peaceful methods. But the conservatives were just as sure they were the victors, that they had won the vote in spite of militancy.

To the impartial observer, however, the argument could have but one answer. Both factions were needed in bringing the struggle to a successful close and both factions must be given the glory of victory.

And now that the long-sought-for right to the ballot was won, women could devote their energies to gaining still other rights.

CHAPTER XX

A "TALKIE" ON WOMEN'S CITIZENSHIP

Women's citizenship had long been a subject of controversy, and in 1907 a law was passed that complicated the problem instead of clarifying it. This law required that women, upon marriage, take the nationality of their husbands. As a result, women born and reared in the United States, women who had never left their native land, lost their American citizenship if they married foreigners.

A most distressing and humiliating loss; for these women were denied property rights; they were denied the vote in states where women had been enfranchisd; if they went abroad for a visit they had no right to the protection of the American consuls because they were no longer Americans; and upon their return to the United States they could be denied entrance on the ground that they were foreigners; they could even be deported as aliens.

But American men could marry women of any foreign country and continue to enjoy all the privileges of American citizenship. Furthermore, foreign women who married American men at once took on American citizenship with all its attendant advantages.

American-born women resented such discrimination, and for a long time they had been working individually and through organizations to change the law. The matter was of vital interest to Ellen Spencer Mussey professionally because she had had difficulties in settling claims cases for American women married to foreigners; had found out that these women could not collect damages as American citizens because they were no longer American citizens. As chairman of the committee on the legal status of women for the National Council of Women, Mrs. Mussey drew up a citizenship bill which was introduced in Congress by Miss Jeanette Rankin, of Montana, first woman in Congress.

The bill provided that American women who married foreigners should retain their citizenship unless they formally renounced it and followed the necessary procedure to do so, and provided that women who had lost their citizenship through marriage should be allowed to regain it.

A hearing was held in December, 1917, before the Committee of Immigration and Naturalization of the House of Representatives. It lasted two days. The World War was being waged, and the question of women's citizenship had suddenly taken on new complications. Among congressmen at the hearing were Harold Knutson, of Minnesota; John E. Raker, of California; James C. Wilson, of Texas; Jacob E. Meeker, of Missouri, and Benjamin F. Welty, of Ohio.

Women representing numerous organizations pleaded in behalf of the bill and the congresswoman, Miss Rankin, opened the discussion:

Miss Rankin—In working for suffrage we have found what a disadvantage it is that women have not their own nationality. For instance, in Montana, which is on the border line of Canada, we found many women this year who could not vote although they had been born in Montana and had lived there all their lives and had never been out of the state . . . they had married Canadians who had not secured naturalization papers.

We have also had the subject arise in relation to land matters where women had taken land and wanted to marry Canadians and could not do so because, in marrying them, these women would lose the land they had, and they had to wait until they had proved up on their land. Of course Canadians do not seem like foreigners to us in Montana because we go back and forth across the line so much.

In the address of the President he said that women would be treated as alien enemies, and according to our law, German women who have married American men cannot be treated as aliens, and no matter how short a time they have lived in America, after marrying American men, they are American citizens, while American women who have married foreigners will be treated as alien enemies. So it is a very serious question right now and it is very unjust at all times that women should not have their own citizenship.

Mr. Knutson—The purpose of this bill, as I understand it, is to allow the American woman to "eat her cake and still have it."

Miss Rankin—No. We submit an American man has the right to citizenship, regardless of marriage, and that the woman has the same right.

Mr. Knutson—As I understand it, the women always take the citizenship of their husbands in every country.

Miss Rankin—No. Not in Australia.

Mr. Knutson—Australia is not a separate country.

Miss Rankin—In Australia a woman has her own citizenship.

Mr. Knutson—It is a portion of Great Britain. Further, do you not think this bill is dangerous?

Miss Rankin—I think it is very dangerous not to pass it.

Mr. Knutson—Have you thought of this feature of it, Miss Rankin, and have your cohorts also thought of it, that here is a German spy and a German enemy of this country who was married to a multimillionaire American, and what is your view as to arranging it so that she can keep the property and at the same time not secretly and quietly furnish these millions to her husband to assist in destroying the boys of our country when we are at war, as we are now, with Germany or Austria?

Miss Rankin—Of course, there would be many problems which would come up under this bill that would need readjustment. . . . I think that the foreign woman who has married an American man and comes here is just as dangerous as the foreign man who marries an American woman, and I think they should be treated as individuals, as human beings, and that we should not separate them as men and women.

Mr. Raker—You know I have heard it discussed ever since a young man, heard it discussed in platforms and every way, about how our rich girls marry the foreigners. This was before we were in war. I was always wondering and I felt hurt that these rich women in the East did not come out to your state and mine and marry some good boys whom we know make such splendid citizens and help build up the country and I know you are with me on that.

Miss Rankin—I think if the men were more attractive the women would marry them.

Mr. Knutson—Why does not the average American woman who desires to marry a foreigner make it a condition of marriage that he become an American citizen?

Miss Rankin—Sometimes she cannot.

Mr. Knutson—Why can she not?

Miss Rankin—Well, because the men are stubborn.

Statement of Mrs. Ellen Spencer Mussey

Mrs. Mussey—I want to say, first of all, that I do not approve at all of American women going outside for their husbands. But that is not a crime and it ought not to prohibit her from retaining her nationality. If a man goes to jail for certain crimes you take away his vote, but it is not a crime to marry a foreigner; not yet.

We have a privileged class of women who are foreigners and whose husbands are American men. We will say she was brought up with German traditions and her husband is an American. He brings her in here and she instantly becomes an American citizen. What do you think about that? She bears the children and she brings them up as Germans in their traditions. I can point to you the cases right here in Washington of where the husbands of German wives wore their iron rings sent by the Kaiser until the war was declared and they were afraid to wear them. I can point to you children in the public schools, brought up by German mothers, who were automatically naturalized right here and brought into this country by Americans, and they have been brought up as Germans and every teacher in the public schools watches these cases. Did not one tell me the other day, "Oh! I make that boy—he is 14 now—write all kinds of essays on citizenship and what the duty of an American citizen is. I am bringing him up as best I can an American citizen but his mother is German and she has brought him up to this age as a German." Is that a right and just law?

Mr. Knutson—Do you realize that even though we passed this law that the country of which the protected woman is not a citizen would not recognize it?

Mrs. Mussey—I certainly do. . . . And this effort is not confined to this country. It is an international effort. There are seven countries where the women are endeavoring to have the passage of this same thing effected; . . . to have the right to retain their nationality, though married to a foreigner.

Mr. Raker—Have you thought of the other side of the question: That if the woman who has married a foreigner could retain her citizenship, as provided for in this bill, and she went abroad, of course she would be an American citizen and her husband would be a citizen of Germany, for instance, as to the complications internationally we would be in, and it would be this country's duty to protect her abroad in the home of her own husband. Have you given that feature of it consideration?

Mrs. Mussey—Yes, and I do not presume that you are just entering on smooth and rosy paths in doing this; and we are ready to help you to work out the difficulties.

Mr. Wilson—Are the majority of the people supposed to find relief under this bill, the American women who have married foreigners and who live abroad?

Mrs. Mussey—No. In this country we are most interested in that. . . . You understand that Miss Rankin said thousands of women are disfranchised under the present conditions. They have married aliens, men waiting for final papers, and yet they cannot exercise the right of franchise.

Mr. Wilson—Why have these men not become American citizens?

Mrs. Mussey—That takes five years. Why should a woman wait five years when you can make an honest law about this thing.

Mrs. Mussey—I want to point out some of the legal disabilities of the woman who is an alien under the present law. In the District of Columbia and in all the territories under the Federal Law, she cannot hold any real estate whatever. You all know that; and, of course the same disability is in certain of the states. There are a great many other things that the alien cannot do. We had a case here of a very wealthy widow who married a young man from a foreign country, who had not been naturalized, and she became an alien. In less than a month her mother passed away leaving a large property, and she was named as executrix. Under our law, an executor must be a citizen of the United States, and she could not be. She lost all of the profit and importance of that office because she had married an alien. . . . If I had unfortunately married an alien, I would not be allowed to practice before the bar of the Supreme Court of the District of Columbia or anywhere else in this country because I would be an alien.

Mr. Knutson—Do you not think this bill is an inducement for further American girls to marry foreigners?

Mrs. Mussey—I do not think so.

Mr. Knutson—They lose absolutely nothing by marrying a foreigner. She becomes "Countess So-and-So." Under this law she could still remain a countess and yet be an American citizen?

Mrs. Mussey—I think she ought not to have the title. I am very glad to have it in the bill that they should not keep the title.

Statement of Mrs. Kate Waller Barrett

Mrs. Barrett— . . . I hope that love is stronger than any law you can pass, and that a woman when she loves a man will marry him in spite of the fact that he is a foreigner. I believe in international marriages. I do not believe there is today anything that is going to help harmonize humanity as much as the marriages that will come out of this war. I believe that the more Canadians who marry, both boys and girls, across the line, the better for American principles. So I am not opposed to the right kind of marriages. Women who go and sell themselves for a title might sell themselves even cheaper if you tempt them.

Mr. Meeker—What would you think about international marriages with Japanese and Chinese?

Mrs. Barrett—So far as I am concerned I do not believe in indiscriminate international marriages. For myself I am Anglo-Saxon, and I would not marry anybody who was not an Anglo-Saxon; but I do not say that is the highest ideal . The time may come when we will be very ashamed of the Anglo-Saxon, because a higher type of humanity has developed. . . .

I want to speak particularly of the hardship that comes to a woman who does not know she has married a foreigner. . . . One of these cases which came before the Bureau of Naturalization has been that of a woman who married a man, thinking him an American citizen. He had gone through the process; he was a voter in three states in which she lived with him, and of course it never entered her head that he was not an American citizen. This man took her abroad and when she came back to this country she was denied admittance. That case went on for three years and it cost that woman almost everything she had in order that she might be permitted to live in this country where her boy and girl were American citizens under the American flag.

Mrs. Barrett—I see a great many of our boys going abroad. Do you mean to say that these men, 200,000 of them, may come back and bring 200,000 French girls with them that they chose to marry and give them full citizenship, when if I should want to marry one of my own friends, I would lose citizenship? Do you think that is just consideration?

Mr. Raker—Taking for granted the kind and character of men who are going abroad to fight for this country and for democracy and liberty and humanity, I believe if they marry in France they will select helpmates that can be and ought to be American citizens.

Mrs. Barrett—There is no one who honors the American soldier more than I. I have the honor of three stars, and I would be perfectly willing to receive as my daughter anyone my son married. At the same time I still maintain that the fact of a woman's marrying a man, whether a soldier or not, is not the reason she should be given citizenship.

STATEMENT OF MISS KATE DEVEREAUX BLAKE, NEW YORK CITY

Miss Blake— . . . You are looking at this from a purely masculine standpoint, from the standpoint of the man who is safe in his citizenship, not from the standpoint of the human being who is weighing even-handed justice—"How would I feel were I in that woman's place?" You have your citizenship; we love ours. . . .

Mr. Raker—Is it not clear, open, broad daylight, voluntary surrender of citizenship when a native-born American girl marries a foreigner?

Miss Blake—Yes, if you make it voluntary renunciation of citizenship of a native-born American man if he marries a foreign woman; not unless. Your question was that it might break up homes. The present law breaks up homes. I know an American girl who has divorced a German husband so that she might not be considered an alien enemy. She expects to remarry him after the war.

Statement of Miss Mary Wood, Representing the General Federation of Women's Clubs

Miss Wood—The plain women of this country, for whom I am going to speak, who have married foreign laborers that help to develop this country and on whom we depend so largely today to maintain the industries which are necessary to keep this nation where it is today, at the head of the whole world, what about them? . . . The American woman married to a foreigner who may retain her citizenship has an immense power with that husband to cajole, to coerce, and to gently lead him into American citizenship. We claim that she will use that power, and that it will be of the greatest benefit to us, especially in these times of stress, when we cannot afford to let any foreign laborer escape. We need them; we need their help; we need their loyalty; . . . and we believe that the foreigner will be induced the more readily to become naturalized.

Mrs. Barrett—I want to bring out a point that was brought out yesterday, and that is the matter of property. If a woman who is an American citizen owns property, it is under the control of the American government, and it belongs to the American woman. Why should it be under the control of a foreign government simply because she has married a foreigner? I say it is one of the most unjust things in the world.

Mr. Welty—Would not that be a good lesson to our American girls to marry American boys?

Mrs. Barrett—There would be fewer international marriages if the American girl did not have the right to give her money to her husband and if it was protected by the laws of this country.

Statement of Mrs. Myra Kingman Miller, President of the National Federation of College Women

Mrs. Miller— . . . If you oppose this bill you are discriminating in citizenship, which is directly contrary to our Constitution. . . . I think the law should be just and should be equal to both men and women in every country.

Mr. Raker—Then your theory is that the law now that naturalizes the woman by virtue of her marriage to an American citizen is wrong?

Mrs. Miller—Wrong.

Mr. Raker—And she should not become a citizen until she has lived here five years and has obtained her naturalization papers? Would not that put an extraordinary burden upon these women who marry American citizens?

Mrs. Miller— . . . You put the same burden on the men. We say now that aliens must know our naturalization laws and have knowledge that would enable them to be good American citizens before we give them citizenship. Why should we discriminate against the man in favor of the woman. They are intelligent human beings. Why should they not be treated so, on an equality?

Statement of Mrs. Alice Park

Mrs. Park—The discussion that I have heard here has been largely devoted to women who have married for title or social position. I think the position of the woman who has no money, and perhaps no education, certainly no landed property or title, deserves special notice. That has come to my attention, and that has worked many hardships in individual cases. We know that when people apply for relief as paupers now in any of the institutions of the states, or for pensions under the new mothers' pension laws, that the various localities enter into an investigation immediately to try to dodge the responsibility, and if they can prove that that person belongs in another country or another state they are very glad to shift the responsibility to avoid the expense to their locality. If they can find that this particular woman married an alien man, no matter how many years ago, and has taken no legal steps to change her status, and has thought nothing of her legal status until that moment, they deny her this relief. . . . I think we should give a great deal more attention in these discussions to the very poor than we do to the very rich.

Statement of Mrs. W. R. Thomas, of Chicago, Ill.

Mr. Raker—Have you any distinction or any preference as to which parent the child's future citizenship should be controlled by?

Mrs. Thomas— . . . It seems to me that the interest of the child should generally be tied up with those of the mother because the mother is the permanent parent. The father is the casual parent. We have developed in Chicago a social term which we apply to the men who desert their families and afterwards come back. We call them the "intermittent fathers," and I think the history of society would show that the mother is the permanent parent. I believe that if the child's citizenship has to be tied up with anybody, it should be tied with the one on whom he can most surely depend.

Mr. Welty—I want to ask Miss Rankin a question. Suppose a woman marries a foreigner and, say, moves to France or Germany or any of the foreign countries; do you think this bill should be drafted in such a way that that woman, if she continued to reside in that country, shall continue to remain an American citizen?

Miss Rankin—I think the law should apply exactly to the woman as it does to the man. If an American man marries a foreign woman and goes to Germany and lives fifty years, unless he takes his papers out in Germany, when he comes back to the United States he is an

American citizen; and as long as he claims his nationality as American he will be an American, and I think it should apply just the same to the women.

Mr. Welty—That may be true. But in case of naturalized citizens who go to foreign countries the presumption is that if they remain there two years they should cease to be citizens of this country.

Miss Rankin—I think that should apply to men and women alike.

Because of the war and because of the fact that public sentiment had not been fully aroused to the need of it, the Women's Citizenship Bill did not receive favorable consideration at this time. But it was given a great deal of publicity, and women's organizations continued the process of education.

At the close of the war the question received a new impetus from numerous cases which involved American women married to foreigners, particularly those married to Germans. Many of these women suffered great hardships. Some of these cases were brought to the personal attention of congressmen, and special acts were passed restoring the American citizenship of these women, but most of those who suffered from citizenship discriminations received no such assistance and their one hope lay in a change of the law.

More bills were introduced in Congress. Mrs. Mussey and Mrs. Maud Wood Park worked together on one measure. But not until 1922 was a law passed, the Cable Act, giving women certain rights to retain their citizenship regardless of marriage.

The law, however, still contained restrictions relative to the regaining of citizenship, to residence abroad of American women married to foreigners, to the citizenship of children, and to marriage with aliens, ineligible to citizenship. American-born Chinese or Japanese women, citizens by reason of birth, marrying men of their own race who did not happen to be born in the United States, immediately lost their citizenship. A mortifying loss, because these women could be excluded from the land of their birth and could not regain their citizenship except through an annulment of the marriage.

No such limitation was placed upon American-born men. They might marry women of any race and still remain American citizens, still enjoy all the protection of the United States Government.

The question by this time was becoming more complicated internationally because in certain countries women kept their citizenship regardless of marriage, in other countries they were compelled to take the nationality of their husbands, and due to these conflicting laws, there were women who became absolutely stateless upon marriage to a foreigner and there were women who took on a dual nationality, kept their own and were claimed as well by the country of their husbands.

But women in many lands were beginning to work together now to establish equal citizenship rights for all women. And in 1934 the representatives of twenty-one American Republics signed an Equal Nationality Treaty at a meeting in Montevideo. Shortly afterward the treaty was ratified by the United States Senate, and on the same day the President signed the Nationality Bill, giving women equal nationality rights with men. This measure had been passed unanimously by both the House and the Senate, an almost unbelievable triumph for women.

Chapter XXI

DEAN MUSSEY'S GIRLS

As the years passed, financial conditions at the law college improved slightly, and at last it was actually possible to pay salaries to faculty members. But the student body kept growing so rapidly and rents for adequate quarters were becoming so high that the school was still far from monetary security.

It occurred to Miss Gillett, who had succeeded Mrs. Mussey as dean, that it might help some if the college had a home of its own, a building large enough to care for future growth, and accordingly the former residence of the famous agnostic, Robert Ingersoll, 1315 K Street, was purchased.

In many ways this seemed a wise move, but the need of money became more and more urgent. What the school required above all else was an endowment fund, and an endowment fund had been started a few years before but interest in it had languished when a certain rich woman promised the college a large sum of money.

This promise, however, failed to materialize, and the financial outlook became so discouraging that some of the trustees and alumni, frantically seeking a solution to the problem, advocated closing the school and turning over whatever funds remained to George Washington University, formerly Columbian College.

Mrs. Mussey was up in arms at once. True, there had been a time when she longed for the deliverance that failure of this school would bring, but not now. For the college had made a place for itself, and most assuredly she would not submit to giving any of its funds to a university that had so persistently refused women the opportunity to study law.

Vigorously she began a campaign to raise a substantial endowment. And alumni, hundreds of them, grateful for the advantages the college had given them, rallied to her support. Even relatives of alumni, proud of what a mother or grandmother had done in the law, sent in contributions. And at last the school had the beginning of a solid foundation.

It kept growing, too. Soon it had fairly overflowed the famous agnostic's residence, and a larger building had to be sought. But the two aging founders had difficulty in agreeing on its selection. Miss Gillett wanted a central location. Mrs. Mussey chose a fine old house in the western part of the city. In the end Mrs. Mussey won, and the new home with its enlargement and improvement became her pride and joy. She loved just to go and look at it. It was her own living monument.

With the new home came a new dean, Mrs. Grace Hays Riley, a graduate of the school. Though the constitution held no ruling on the subject, it had become the unwritten law that the school head should be a woman. Nor did this policy in any way discourage men students, for every year brought more of them; and when Mrs. Riley became dean, her husband, Major J. Garfield Riley, enrolled as a student.

Mrs. Mussey exulted at this. Here, indeed, was the very culmination of proof that men did not object to studying law with women. And Mrs. Mussey was proud of her "boys." They did excellent work as students and they went forth to creditable records in the profession.

But of course there was nothing new or unusual about this, for men had been going to law schools for centuries and countless numbers of them had made excellent records and gone forth to renown at the bar.

Women, though—hedged about for ages upon ages by prejudice and discrimination because of their sex, barred from the study of law and the practice of law, forced even in modern times to battle with the absurdities of tradition—their accomplishments in the law were of profound significance. Jubilantly, Mrs. Mussey watched over the unfolding careers of her girls.

Because they were making new records. They were not only winning success before the bar but they were going into fields never before entered by women, they were piling up a long list of firsts for their sex.

There was Miss Caroline Griesheimer, the first woman to be detailed as Civil Service Examiner; Miss Adele Stewart, the first woman to be appointed National Bank Examiner; Miss Pearl McCall, the first woman Assistant United States District Attorney in the District of Columbia; Miss Agnes O'Neil, the first woman Assistant Solicitor of the Department of State; Mrs. Flora Warren Seymour, the first woman on the Board of Indian Commissioners; Miss A. Viola Smith, the first woman appointed as American Trade Commissioner; Miss Annabel Matthews, the first woman on the United States Board of Tax Appeals; Miss Alice M. Birdsall, the first woman to be reporter of the supreme court of a state, appointed to this office in Arizona; and Miss Katharine Pike, the first woman of the law in the United States Customs Service and the first woman to go to sea as a customs officer.

Miss Pike's experience typified the attitude toward women in new jobs. She wanted to be a customs examiner and was working up to this position when the edict was given out that in the future none except law school graduates would be appointed as examiners. So Miss Pike went to the law school founded for women, finished the three-year course in two years with honors, and shortly afterward became a customs examiner.

A most dangerous job for a woman, it was said, because customs examiners must board ships at sea. But Miss Pike, boarding the *Kaiserin Victoria* from a revenue cutter for her first inspection, found this a minor incident in the performance of her duty and no more hazardous than many of the traditional tasks of womankind. Of course one might fall into the sea; but then, one might also get blown up starting fire in the kitchen stove; and one might fall down one's own stairway and suffer a broken neck.

At the time of the sugar frauds, Miss Pike inspected scales in the warehouses of the port of New York, another new job for a woman, and therefore alarming. Gossip was rampant that women were to do all the inspecting in the future, that men were not to be trusted with the job.

As the years passed, Miss Pike became an authority on customs. When Warren G. Harding was elected President, he appointed Elmer Dover, Assistant Secretary of the Treasury, to be in charge of customs and internal revenue. And Mr. Dover, seeking help on customs problems, went to John Corwin, of the Customs Division, and asked for the man who had the most thorough knowledge of the subject.

"H——," exclaimed the outspoken Mr. Corwin, "it's not a man. It's a woman. Her name's Pike."

A woman, indeed! Mr. Dover was skeptical. But after an investigation he made Miss Pike his assistant, and she was given a raise of a thousand dollars in salary.

Dean Mussey's girls could write on legal matters, too. One of the subjects difficult to teach in the law school had been common law pleading, but when Miss Helen Jamison, of Iowa, became a student at the college she revealed such remarkable ability on the subject that the faculty asked her to write a textbook. She complied, perhaps the first woman ever to write a textbook on law. Mrs. Nanette B. Paul also turned her attention to writing and became an authority on parliamentary law.

By the second decade of the twentieth century, women had made places for themselves in many branches of the legal profession but no women were sitting on the bench. The world's congenital aversion to something new must still be reckoned with, for in spite of the fact that Deborah had been an able judge over the Israelites and long past eras may have produced other women jurists, such magistracies were too rare and too hazy with antiquity to have meaning for a practical and dubious people. But the way was being paved to this accomplishment.

In 1918 the third term of the Juvenile Court Judgeship in the District of Columbia expired and, as formerly, the President nominated a man. But the Senate did not confirm this nomination.

A strategic time, then, for the consideration of a woman. Mrs. Mussey was now sixty-eight and past the eligible age, and few women were willing to try for such a post, but those interested in the appointment of a woman finally found a candidate in the person of Miss Kathryn Sellers, one of Dean Mussey's girls, a native of Marysville, Ohio, librarian and bibliographer for the Carengie Peace Foundation, and a dollar-a-year employee of the Department of State. A calm, trustworthy, forceful woman, well-fitted for the Juvenile Court, her friends believed. In due time she was asked to call upon the Attorney General for an interview.

But Miss Sellers had no political acquaintance and apparently little chance to win. She herself had no expectations, and her brother said, "Don't even tell anyone that you are being considered, for you will never be appointed."

The great drama of the World War was on, however, women had achieved a new status, they were being accepted readily in many new positions, and the President, Woodrow Wilson, sent Miss Sellers' name to the Senate.

Letters of recommendation came pouring in, and opposition to the appointment was practically negligible. As a result, in September, 1918, the Senate confirmed the nomination.

And Washington, D. C., forty-five years after acceptance of its first woman of the law, had its first woman on the bench. Miss Sellers was the first woman in the country to be judge of a juvenile court, the first woman to be appointed to the bench under Federal authority.

A victory, this, for women and a victory for the law school that had been founded for women. A grave responsibility, too, because Miss Sellers must prove women's fitness for the bench. With a solicitude that was both professional and maternal, Dean Mussey hurried to an early session of Judge Sellers' court to see that her former student was fulfilling all the requirements.

The Judge of the Juvenile Court did not sit on a lofty bench, but occupied a more informal position in a swivel chair at a desk, and Mrs. Mussey sat near the Judge. As soon as the session ended, Judge Sellers turned to Dean Mussey for her verdict.

"You did fine!" exclaimed Mrs. Mussey, "but Kathryn," the Dean lowered her voice to a whisper, "pull your skirt down in the back. Your legs show."

"I don't dare," the Judge whispered back, "for if I do, it will pull up in front."

Skirts were tight but by no means as short as they were to become some years later, and it was considered most immodest for a woman to reveal her legs. And for a woman judge to do so was the very height of impropriety. It would be sure to bring unfavorable reaction to women in office and something had to be done about it.

But Judge Sellers solved the problem. She had a special skirt made to wear in court. And since her desk had an opening through the center, she took still further precaution to conceal her legs, by having a little curtain put over this opening.

At the end of her term, Judge Sellers was reappointed for another six years.

Quite naturally now, other women were seeking judgeships. One of them was Miss Mary O'Toole, blue-eyed daughter of Ireland, who had come to America and Hammondsport, N. Y., as a young girl. Her advent into the law was typical. As court reporter for Steuben County, she took readily to legal matters, and when one aged lawyer frequently made mistakes in his papers, she corrected them. One day he said to her, "Why don't you study law?"

"I'm going to," replied "Molly" O'Toole.

She went to Washington, D. C., got a job as government clerk, and enrolled at Mrs. Mussey's and Miss Gillett's school because that was the only school for white persons that admitted women. When she had completed her college course, Miss O'Toole, at the age of thirty-eight, began the practice of law in Washington.

But it was difficult getting a foothold in the profession, and one day when she was low in spirits she said to Dean Mussey, "I started to practice law too late."

"Molly, sit down here," commanded the Dean. "I want to talk to you. I was forty-two years old when my husband died. I thought life was all over for me but I lived to learn it was all before me." And Dean Mussey recounted her own struggles.

Encouraged, Molly O'Toole went to work. In order to widen her circle of acquaintances, she joined women's clubs, allied herself with Chamber of Commerce work, and woman suffrage activities. Soon she was becoming known and she had plenty of law cases.

Mrs. Mussey was very fond of Molly O'Toole and had high hopes for her future. When one of the judges of the municipal court resigned in 1921 Mrs. Mussey decided that Molly was the very person for the post.

The latter, however, was reluctant to be a candidate because she was sure she could not win. But Mrs. Mussey insisted, and presently Miss O'Toole, though she was still certain she could not be appointed, began to ask a few friends and acquaintances for recommendations.

Then the public heard that a woman was seeking an appointment to the municipal bench and all at once it seemed everybody was talking about it. Miss O'Toole had not expected so much publicity, and it occurred to her suddenly that, with everyone knowing about her candidacy, she could not bear to fail.

Setting to work in earnest, she conferred with Republican leaders, visited government officials, and called upon everyone who might have some favorable bearing on her appointment. It was an endless round, for obtaining interviews with public men was extremely difficult. They disliked especially to be bothered by a woman. She had to telephone the office of Attorney General Daugherty thirteen times before she succeeded in getting an appointment with him.

And opposition to her candidacy was strong, not because she lacked ability but because she was a woman. Judge Michael Doyle, who had left the post she sought, gave heated vent to his objections. Such jobs should be given to men, he contended; that there were not enough places as it was for men; and he refused absolutely to indorse her candidacy.

It was noised about, too, that Judge Gould, of the Supreme Court of the District of Columbia, was in a fury because a woman had been suggested for this place. He was a friend of President Harding and the story was told that in a conference with the President on the matter, the Judge strode up and down the south portico of the White House and raged, "A woman on the municipal bench will belittle the job, will belittle every one of us."

Others, however, insisted that Molly O'Toole was the best "man" for the job, and when President Harding made inquiries as to her acceptability among the business people, she was highly recommended. In July, 1921, her name was sent to the Senate and confirmation soon followed.

But certain men of the bar seriously objected, and they vowed they would never try a case before a woman. Some of them were present at her first session of court. Out of curiosity, perhaps. And they found that Judge O'Toole was a capable, smiling, judicious woman. By the end of the session most of the hostility had been dispelled, and men who had been the most antagonistic were among those who came up to offer congratulations on her appointment.

Even Judge Doyle, who had been so opposed to having a woman successor, became her friend, and when she was up for a second term four years later he offered his indorsement. She was reappointed without difficulty.

Other women, too, were winning judgeships. In 1921 Florence E. Allen was elected Judge of the Court of Common Pleas in Cuyahoga County, Ohio, the first woman in the United States to be elected judge. Though Florence Allen was not a student at Mrs. Mussey's school, she was, in a way, one of Mrs. Mussey's girls just the same. Mrs. Mussey's father, Platt Spencer, and Florence Allen's grandfather, Jacob Tuckerman, were great friends, and the latter's family watched the development of Ellen Spencer Mussey's career with interest.

As Florence Allen grew up, her mother told her over and over again of the achievements of Mrs. Mussey and pointed to her pridefully as an example. Not many young girls had such a model held up to them, and Florence Allen was deeply impressed. She resolved that she, too, would be a lawyer. And her success was marked.

She became a judge of the Supreme Court of Ohio, the first woman on the bench of the supreme court of a state, and later she was appointed to the bench of the United States Circuit Court of Appeals, the first woman to sit on the bench of a major Federal court. In 1934 Judge Allen was given the honorary degree of Doctor of Laws by the college which Mrs. Mussey had helped found and over which she had worked and struggled so many years.

Often women seeking places on the bench encountered almost hopeless obstacles. In Macon, Missouri, in 1922, Miss Albirtie Wright sought election as judge of the Probate Court of Macon County. She had been clerk of this court and had gone to Washington, D. C., as secretary to its former judge, M. A. Romjue, who had been elected to Congress. After studying law at the school founded for women, Miss Wright went back to Macon and entered the primaries.

But she was defeated. Macon County wanted no woman as judge. In fact it was so prejudiced against women it had even opposed woman suffrage. No woman except Miss Wright had ever run for office in this county and no woman had ever practiced law there. But Miss Wright studied more law in Washington, D. C., returned to Macon, took up the practice of law, and in 1926 was again a candidate for the Probate Court. Opposing her in the primaries were two men, the incumbent, and one of Macon's well-known bankers. But Miss Wright won the nomination this time, and in November she was elected, the first woman in Missouri to be elected Probate Judge, though in two other counties women had been appointed to this office.

These judgeships were triumphs for Mrs. Mussey. But she knew they were merely the beginning of woman's success in the law, that women were still pioneering. And she visioned the day when the world, grown more mature, would no longer oppose women on the grounds of sex, but give them full opportunity for development and accept them as judges in the highest tribunal of the land, the United States Supreme Court, as well as in all other high elective and appointive offices.

Dreams! The dreams of an old lady who had already passed her three score years and ten. But what miracles had been wrought in those years, what incredible changes had come to pass in woman's sphere! And more were still to come. Hopefully, enthusiastically, Mrs. Mussey looked toward the future.

CHAPTER XXII

EVENING

The passing years brought no dimming of Ellen Spencer Mussey's zest for social life. Dinners, luncheons, club meetings, receptions—how she loved them! And to go to the White House, to meet the President and First Lady, to mingle with the other guests invited there, was for her the greatest of pleasures.

An ardent Republican, she was delighted when Warren G. Harding, of Ohio, became President. The Hardings gave many receptions, and Mr. Harding, a tall, handsome man and a genial host, captivated her. Mrs. Harding, too, was a satisfying hostess. She always asked about the law school. One day she said to Mrs. Mussey, "When I get through this job, I'm coming over to your college to study law."

Mrs. Mussey took her granddaughter to meet Mrs. Harding and was given the privilege of showing the young woman about the second floor of the White House where General Mussey had had his office as military secretary to President Johnson and where Miss Surratt had come to plead for her mother, accused in the assassination of Abraham Lincoln.

And Mrs. Mussey took her twelve-year-old grandson to a White House lawn party to shake hands with Mr. Harding. The President was so cordial to old and young alike that the lad was greatly impressed and he remarked with youthful seriousness, "If Mr. Harding is as much of a success politically as he is socially, he'll make a fine President."

Mrs. Mussey heartily agreed. She wanted Mr. Harding to succeed. And when his regime had ended in tragedy and ill repute, she found it difficult to lay any blame upon Mr. Harding. He was weak, she said, and he had been the victim of unscrupulous friends.

The Coolidges came to the White House, and Mrs. Mussey met a gracious new hostess. It was fairly easy, particularly for people of distinction or social prominence, to be received at the Executive Mansion if they asked that favor, and Mrs. Coolidge generously received people from all walks of life. Mrs. Mussey wanted to introduce her granddaughter to Mrs. Coolidge and when the young lady was in Washington for the Christmas holidays she and Mrs. Mussey were invited to the White House for tea on the afternoon before Christmas.

Mrs. Coolidge entertained many Washingtonians and their out-of-town visitors in this manner, and at the Christmas tea there were perhaps twenty guests, including several college girls.

They were ushered into one of the White House parlors to wait until Mrs. Coolidge should be ready to receive them in the next room, a procedure to be expected. But one elderly guest, a woman of an old and established family, resented this delay. She refused to be kept waiting by anyone, and insisted upon going at once to greet Mrs. Coolidge. An attendant, however, gently but firmly averted this action.

It greatly annoyed this guest, too, that so many other people were there with her. She was used to being received alone, she told Mrs. Mussey. Mrs. Harding had received her alone, and she could not understand why Mrs. Coolidge had not done likewise. When the group was admitted to the next parlor, the first to greet Mrs. Coolidge was this elderly guest and she clung fast to her opportunity. She asked Mrs. Coolidge about her health; she asked about the President's health; she inquired at length about the two Coolidge boys; then, quite as if no one else was waiting, she went into details about the welfare of her own family, all the while Mrs. Coolidge was graciously indicating the direction of the tea table. But this guest must have her say.

At another White House tea, Mrs. Mussey was accompanied by her daughter. The latter wished to meet Mr. Coolidge, but he did not attend the teas. She saw him one morning, however, when he was out walking with his son and had a vivid glimpse of one of the much-talked of Presidential characteristics.

A man greeted Mr. Coolidge.

"Who was that?" asked his son.

"Mr. ———, an F Street merchant," answered the President. Then, as if recalling numerous gowns, slippers, and accessories that Mrs. Coolidge had bought at this merchant's store, the President added regretfully, "He costs me lots of money."

Such incidents as these Mrs. Mussey treasured, and she liked to look back over the years and recall all her varied experiences with the people and events of the White House from the time when, as one of a mad scrambling throng at a public reception, she had had her first visit there in the days of the Grants, to the times when she and General Mussey had called upon Mr. and Mrs. Hayes and Mr. and Mrs. Garfield, and the more formal times when she went to the White House with delegations to seek the President's approval of some project.

But she was not sitting down yet to live in her memories. Too many things were still to be done. There were still too many legal discriminations against women. Even her own act of 1896 had left women of the District of Columbia with a tremendous handicap. Though it had given the mother the same rights as the father in the child and had given married women the right to their own earnings, it had not given married women the right to act as surety, guarantor, accommodation drawer, or indorser for another. Few women felt this need in 1896 because few women were in business, but later, as increasing numbers of them entered the business field, this restriction became formidable.

Also it brought difficulties upon the banks. For married women sometimes borrowed money for the benefit of their husbands and took advantage of the law to avoid payment. In one case a woman borrowed a large sum of money for her husband, gave as security collateral owned by herself, and when the note fell due, refused to pay. The bank brought suit, but the court decided, in full accord with the law, that a married woman had no right to make such a contract and therefore was not legally responsible for the debt. The bank could not collect.

After that, banks were extremely cautious in loaning money to married women, and this policy limited business for the banks as well as married women. At last, in 1926, a concerted effort was made to change the law. Mrs. Mussey was asked to help. With representatives of the banks, members of the District Bar Association and the Women's Bar Association, she went to a hearing before a committee of Congress.

Though one southern congressman ventured to protest, "This bill is a dangerous thing. We must protect our wives," the need of a new law was so obvious that no real difficulty was encountered, and the measure was soon passed.

Women of the District were now asking for still another right—to serve on juries. And they were being greeted with all the arguments that had once been used against woman suffrage: that woman's sex debarred her; that her place was in the home; that she had not the mentality for such a task; that she was too emotional. The opponents, themselves, in a veritable froth of emotionalism, fought jury service for women.

But women were insistent. As citizens and taxpayers, as individuals subject to the law, they demanded the rights and benefits of their own sex in the jury box. Only in this way, they maintained, could there be even-handed justice.

Congress was wrestling with a jury service bill. Organized women were lobbying for the measure. And Mrs. Mussey, taking advantage of her acquaintance with congressmen, urged its passage. At every opportunity she talked jury service for women.

In 1927 a law was passed. But it was a spineless thing. It allowed women to be excused from jury service merely upon their request to be excused. Capable, spirited women, laboring to invest their sex with the full responsibilities of citizenship, were indignant. They demanded a law that would read the same for women as for men.

But Mrs. Mussey was cheerful. The new law was at least a step in advance, and she was sure the rest would come. She could be patient, perhaps, because she had seen so much accomplished in women's behalf. But of course, the jury service battle would have to be fought all over again. By younger crusaders, however. Mrs. Mussey was becoming a little tired. Eighty was just around the corner.

Still she kept up some law practice, chiefly the management of estates. And there was the law school. Like a mother superior she watched over its activities, the problem of the growing student body, the expansion of the endowment fund. When the college opened in the fall, she must be there to greet the students, and she liked to attend their social events, particularly the banquets. At the banquet given a few months before her seventy-ninth birthday she was as usual a speaker on the program.

Meticulously she made ready for this event, for she always wanted to look her best for her students. Some one had to come from the beauty shop to curl and arrange her hair; she had a new dress of soft gray silk; and sheer hose and slippers though she was accustomed to wearing high, warm shoes. It was a cold February night, too, but she was blithely sure she would not take cold.

Her speech was brief and witty, with anecdotes of the early days of the college when women who studied law were "queer," when one young woman, to hide the shamful fact that she was so bold as to study law, had registered under an assumed name.

A long past era was this, with all its attendant prejudices, and Mrs. Mussey, sitting down amidst the warm applause, gazed feelingly about the crowded banquet room at the young women who could take their law studies as a matter of course and the young men who so matter-of-factly attended the same law classes. It seemed strange to Mrs. Mussey now that she and Miss Gillett should have been so hesitant about founding a law school. Yet they could not have dreamed of the success that was to come.

But Miss Gillett was gone now. She could no longer share in the victory, no longer enjoy the plaudits of the grateful students. At seventy-nine, Mrs. Mussey mused wistfully, so many comrades, so many loved ones, have departed.

She always went home early now. She needed to conserve her strength, to have the solitude of her apartment, the ease of a loose-flowing dressing gown.

And she lived alone. Miss Lizzie, constant companion for nearly fifty years, was gone, children and grandchildren lived in other cities. But Washington was Mrs. Mussey's home. Her work and her friends were there.

Sometimes there were protests against this aloneness. "But I'm much better off this way," she would insist briskly. The comfort of independence! A maid to come in and keep things clean; meals carefully prescribed at a diet home close by, with men and women of the government as companions; discussions, work, varied interests; folks, many of them young people, coming to call; parties; life went along smoothly, busily, and happily.

But time was taking its toll. Her eyesight was failing. For years she had worn spectacles and now she must use a reading glass. Even then, it was difficult to see. Sometimes folks read to her, but that was never enough. One evening, a friend, finding her worn out with tired aching eyes, chided, "You've been reading too much again."

"Yes," Mrs. Mussey admitted, "but there are so many interesting things going on that I want to know about."

In her enthusiasm for life she was inclined to overdo just as she had done in the days of her youth and middle age. A few months before her eightieth birthday, she suffered a serious breakdown. There had been too much work, too much society, and then a sudden influx of troubles—a fire at her apartment house, illness in her family, the death of a client with all the attendant worries. For many weeks she was in a hospital and after that a nursing home.

She was oppressed by a vast weariness. Her mind was clouded, her talk confused. It seemed to be the beginning of the end.

But she had weathered many an illness, and with time and the best care available, once again the current of life rallied. She was not to give up yet.

With convalescence came a new honor. In celebration of the tenth anniversary of woman suffrage, the National League of Women Voters, an outgrowth of the National American Woman Suffrage Association, inaugurated a movement toward the recognition of women whose work and achievement had so long been ignored or at best inadequately recorded in history.

The League established a national honor roll to be inscribed with the names of women from every state who had done outstanding work for the advancement of their sex. And in the District of Columbia, Ellen Spencer Mussey was chosen as one to be so honored.

Friends celebrated her selection. At a luncheon, club women and men and women of the bar gave public expression to the esteem in which she was held. Mrs. Mussey was not well enough to attend this event, but the speeches were broadcast and she was presented with a carefully prepared copy of all the glowing tributes to her achievements as a lawyer, an educator, and a reformer.

And this acclaim was like a tonic. Once again life took on renewed interest. She began to sit up for longer periods, to see more people and, when the weather was fine, to go for automobile rides. On the afternoon of her eightieth birthday, May 13, she went into society again. At one of her clubs a party was given in her honor.

There was a huge birthday cake, bearing eighty candles, boxes and boxes of lovely flowers and gifts, and a host of friends and acquaintances. Mrs. Mussey was intensely happy. She blew out her candles and made a little speech of appreciation. The old fire and sparkle were somewhat dimmed because of the long illness, but she was self-possessed and her voice was steady.

She was so pleased to be able to go to parties again, to be among folks, that almost childlike, she planned to make this festivity last as long as possible. She decided not only to stay at the club for the entire party but to remain to dinner as well, to have a meal at a table again. It had become so monotonous eating from trays.

But she was beginning to look tired. So many people, so many felicitations, were exciting, and her physician sent word that "Cinderella" had better go home.

Still she was bent on staying. "Just for soup and salad," she said.

Solicitous friends, however, were firm. She must do as the doctor said. Reluctantly, then, perhaps even a little rebelliously, she yielded, a gray little partridge of a woman, still filled with the urge of life, pathetically losing an inning to time.

But she was soon mistress again. She took charge of matters relating to her law practice, attended to business problems, became active in college affairs, went to more parties. She was her old self. And once again she was received at the White House. Friends arranged a meeting with Mr. Hoover, and she was accompanied by her grandson, now a young man in college.

President Hoover said, "Mrs. Mussey, you've had a long and distinguished career. I'm very glad to meet you."

How proud and happy it made her to have a President say that, particularly in the presence of her grandson.

Summer came. Washington was hot and sultry as of old, and Mrs. Mussey went to the seashore. Save for the coming and going of friends and relatives, she was alone. And because of her recent illness, certain of those close to her remonstrated at this aloneness.

"But I'm all right," she assured them spiritedly. "Besides, there are always physicians, nurses, and folks to help when one needs them."

She busied herself with her practice, made plans for the college, and looked forward to the social life of the fall. Eighty . . . pooh! Life was still absorbing. Gaily, Ellen Spencer Mussey went on with it.

But everything must pass, and Mrs. Mussey was not one to cling absurdly to that which was passing. With the weighing down of the years came a gentle relinquishment of duties and activities. She turned over to others what was left of her law practice; she went to fewer parties; attended fewer college functions.

It had been her custom always to sign the diplomas of each graduating class, and in 1933 she performed this task as usual. But she was very tired after that, almost too tired to go to the commencement exercises. Yet she wanted to be there, felt that she must be there, for this was not only the thirty-fifth annual commencement of her school, but Anna Eleanor Roosevelt, wife of the President, Franklin D. Roosevelt, was to receive the honorary degree of Doctor of Laws and was to be the speaker of the evening.

Mrs. Mussey had gone with Mrs. Grace Hays Riley, Dean of the College, to the White House where they had an appointment with Mrs. Roosevelt to discuss the commencement plans. They found Mrs. Roosevelt most gracious and informal, and Mrs. Mussey was particularly delighted with the way in which Mrs. Roosevelt spoke of her husband. In past visits to the White House, Mrs. Mussey had noted that many First Ladies referred to their husbands with the greatest formality as "the President." But Mrs. Roosevelt, simply and charmingly, called her husband, "Frank."

On the evening of commencement, Mrs. Mussey and Mrs. Roosevelt, side by side, led the march down the aisle of Memorial Continental Hall, Mrs. Mussey a plump gray little woman, worn but proud and happy; Mrs. Roosevelt, tall and smiling, a woman of amazing energy and infinite kindliness. At the foot of the steps to the platform Mrs. Mussey paused, turned to Dr. Edwin C. Dutton, President of the Board of Trustees, and expressed her apprehension at getting safely up the steps.

But Mrs. Roosevelt said quickly, "I'll take care of you," and gently helped Mrs. Mussey to her place on the platform.

On the day after commencement, Mrs. Mussey received a letter of appreciaion from Mrs. Roosevelt for the honor that had been conferred upon her by the college. It was a brief typed letter, but delightful, and Mrs. Mussey observed proudly, "Mrs. Roosevelt signed it herself."

This was Mrs. Mussey's last commencement. She was tired so much of the time now. After a while she remained in her room continuously. And then she required the care of a trained nurse. But she still read or had others read to her, she saw her friends, and discussed the affairs of the day, the progress of the college.

The end came peacefully. She was stricken suddenly, became unconscious, and died a few hours later on the morning of April 21, 1936, less than a month before her eighty-sixth birthday.

She had had a full life, a life of effort and pain, joy and love, service and accomplishment. And now she could rest; she could have that last long lovely sleep.

THE END